OTHER BOOKS BY THE AUTHOR

THE
HIDDEN
OF GO

M.

Le

A

God*

God*

Th

the swans are not silent

BOOK TWO

the Hidden SMILE *of* GOD

The Fruit of Affliction
in the Lives of John Bunyan,
William Cowper, and David Brainerd

JOHN PIPER

CROSSWAY BOOKS • WHEATON, ILLINOIS
A DIVISION OF GOOD NEWS PUBLISHERS

Library of Congress Cataloging-in-Publication Data

Piper, John, 1946-
　　The hidden smile of God: the fruit of affliction in the lives of John
Bunyan, William Cowper, and David Brainerd / John Piper.
　　　　p.　　cm.
　　Includes bibliographical references and indexes.
　　ISBN 1-58134-247-0 (alk. paper)
　　1. Bunyan, John, 1628-1688. 2. Cowper, William, 1731-1800.
3. Brainerd, David, 1718-1747. 4. Christian biography. I. Title.
BR1700.3.P56　2001
270.7'092'2—dc21　　　　　　　　　　　　　　00-011665
　　　　　　　　　　　　　　　　　　　　　　　　　　　CIP

15	14	13	12	11	10	09	08	07	06	05	04	03	02	01
15	14	13	12	11	10	9	8	7	6	5	4	3	2	1

To
George T. Henry[†] and Pamela C. Henry

Parents of my wife,
partners in the warfare,
precious in life and death

CONTENTS

Judge not the Lord by feeble sense,

But trust him for his grace;

Behind a frowning providence

He hides a smiling face.

WILLIAM COWPER

"GOD MOVES IN A MYSTERIOUS WAY"

PREFACE

The swans sing sweetly when they suffer. The swans I have in mind are John Bunyan (1628-1688), William Cowper (1731-1800), and David Brainerd (1718-1747). I call them swans because they are great voices for Christian truth that death has not silenced.

When the unrivaled Augustine, the Bishop of Hippo in North Africa, retired in A.D. 430, he handed over his duties to his humble successor, Eraclius. At the ceremony, Eraclius stood to preach as the aged Augustine sat on his bishop's throne behind him. Overwhelmed by a sense of inadequacy in Augustine's presence, Eraclius said, "The cricket chirps, the swan is silent."[1] This story is the origin of the title for this series of books called *The Swans Are Not Silent*. You are now reading Book Two. The first was called *The Legacy of Sovereign Joy: God's Triumphant Grace in the Lives of Augustine, Luther, and Calvin*.

The reference to swans appeared again a thousand years later. On July 6, 1415, John Hus (whose name in Czech means "goose") was burned at the stake for criticizing the Roman Catholic sale of indulgences. Just before his death, he is said to have written, "Today, you are burning a goose; however, a hundred years from now, you will be able to hear a swan sing; you will not burn it, you will have to listen to him."[2] And so the line of "swans" has continued down to our own day—faithful witnesses to the gospel of the glory of Christ whose death does not silence their song.

---

[1] Peter Brown, *Augustine of Hippo* (Berkeley, CA: University California Press, 1969), p. 408.
[2] Erwin Weber, "Luther with the Swan," *The Lutheran Journal*, vol. 65, no. 2, 1996, p. 10.

My aim in this series of books is to magnify the voice of the
swans with the megaphone of their lives. The apostle Paul calls the
church to "adorn the doctrine of God" with the fidelity of our
lives (Titus 2:10). That is what the swans have done, especially
in their suffering. Their steadfastness through trial sweetens and
intensifies the song of their faith. It is part of our pleasant
Christian duty to preserve and proclaim the faith-sustaining stories of Christ's suffering swans. The Bible exhorts us that we "not
be sluggish, but imitators of those who through faith and patience
inherit the promises" (Hebrews 6:12). "Remember those who
led you, who spoke the word of God to you; and considering the
result of their conduct, imitate their faith" (Hebrews 13:7). But we
can't imitate or be inspired by what we don't know. Hence the
series, *The Swans Are Not Silent*.

The three stories that I tell in this book were originally bio-
graphical messages delivered orally at the Bethlehem Conference
for Pastors. I am influenced in my selection of these three for this
book by the conviction expressed by Benjamin Brook in the pref-
ace to his three-volume work, *The Lives of the Puritans*:

> Of all the books which can be put into your hands, those
> which relate the labors and suffering of good men are the
> most interesting and instructive. In them you see orthodox
> principles, Christian tempers, and holy duties in lovely
> union and in vigorous operation. In them you see religion
> shining forth in real life, subduing the corruptions of
> human nature, and inspiring a zeal for every good work.
> In them you see the reproaches and persecutions which
> the servants of God have endured; those gracious principles
> which have supported their minds; and the course they have
> pursued in their progress to the kingdom of heaven. Such

books are well calculated to engage your attention, to affect your feelings, to deepen your best impressions, and to invigorate your noblest resolutions. They are well calculated to fortify you against the allurements of a vain world; to assimilate your characters to those of the excellent of the earth; to conform your lives to the standard of holiness; and to educate your souls for the mansions of glory.[3]

These are my aims. And I agree that "The labors and suffering of good men are the most interesting and instructive" for these great ends. It is apparent, therefore, that I do not write as a disinterested scholar, but rather as a passionately interested—and I hope honest and careful—pastor whose mission in life is to spread a passion for the supremacy of God in all things for the joy of all peoples.

John Bunyan, William Cowper, and David Brainerd labored and suffered. And it was by this very affliction that they bore fruit for the nourishing of radical Christian living, God-centered worship, and Christ-exalting world missions. How they suffered, how they endured, and how it bore fruit is the story that, I pray, will inspire in you that same radical Christian life, God-centered worship, and Christ-exalting mission.

John Bunyan is best known as the simple, British, Baptist pastor who in prison wrote the book that to this day "remains the widest circulating single piece of literature in the history of the human race outside of the Bible,"[4] *The Pilgrim's Progress*. It is a great book about how to live the Christian life. Lesser known

---

[3] Benjamin Brook, *The Lives of the Puritans*, vol. 1 (Pittsburgh: Soli Deo Gloria Publications, 1994, orig. 1813), pp. vi-vii.

[4] Barry Horner, *The Pilgrim's Progress by John Bunyan, Themes and Issues: An Evangelical Apologetic* (Lindenhurst, NY: Reformation Press Publishing, 1998), p. 2.

is the fact that his twelve years in prison were "voluntary," in the sense that a commitment not to preach the Gospel of Jesus Christ would have obtained his freedom at any time. This fact intensifies the effect of knowing that when Bunyan's oldest child Mary—blind from birth—visited him in prison, it was like "the pulling of the Flesh from my bones."[5] Fewer still are those who know that this imprisoned pastor, with no formal education beyond grammar school, also wrote some sixty other books, most of which are still in print 350 years later.[6]

William Cowper, for those who, along the way, happened to take a course in eighteenth-century literature, is known as "the poet of a new religious revival" led by John Wesley and George Whitefield. His poetry and letters merited fifty pages in the anthology I studied in college.[7] Among those who know him as a Christian poet, many do not know that William Cowper lived with bleak depression as a steady companion all his life, sometimes immobilized in despair, and repeatedly attempting suicide. In spite of this darkness, Cowper today is still touching the hearts of thousands who know nothing of him at all, simply because, in worship, they sing his hymns "There Is a Fountain Filled with Blood," "O for a Closer Walk with God," and "God Moves in a Mysterious Way."

David Brainerd would probably not be known by anyone today if it were not for Jonathan Edwards, the New England pas-

[5] John Bunyan, *Grace Abounding to the Chief of Sinners* (Hertfordshire, England: Evangelical Press, 1978), p. 123.

[6] The "Catalogue-Table of Mr. Bunyan's Books," *The Works of John Bunyan*, vol. 3, George Offor, ed. (Edinburgh: The Banner of Truth Trust, 1991), p. 763, lists sixty works of Bunyan. See also the complete list of his writings in Christopher Hill, *A Tinker and a Poor Man: John Bunyan and His Church, 1628-1688* (New York: Alfred A. Knopf, 1989), pp. xv-xvii.

[7] Louis Bredvold, Alan McKillop, Lois Whitney, eds., *Eighteenth Century Poetry and Prose*, 2nd edition (New York: The Ronald Press Co., 1956), p. 882.

tor, in whose house this young missionary to the American Indians died of tuberculosis when he was twenty-nine. Edwards took Brainerd's diary and turned it into what is called *The Life of David Brainerd*,[8] a biography that has inspired more missionary service, perhaps, than any other book outside the Bible.[9] There were no specialists to tell the twenty-two-year-old Brainerd, when he began to spit blood in his sophomore year at Yale, that he was an unfit candidate for missionary stress in the wilderness. So for the next seven years, after being expelled from Yale, he laid down his life for the salvation of "the Stockbridge, Delaware and Susquehanna Tribes of Indians."[10] His story has become a spiritual classic, and "it is as hard to number the great company seen by John on Patmos as to count that company—red, brown, yellow, and white—brought into the Kingdom of God directly or indirectly by the young consumptive who burned himself out in the wilderness of New York, Pennsylvania, and New Jersey over two centuries ago."[11]

---

[8] The full title of the 1749 edition was *An Account of the Life of the late Reverend Mr. David Brainerd, Minister of the Gospel, Missionary to the Indians, from the honourable Society in Scotland, for the Propagation of Christian Knowledge, and Pastor of a Church of Christian Indians in New Jersey. Who died at Northampton in New England, October 9th, 1747, in the 30th year of his Age: Chiefly taken from his own Diary, and other private Writings, written for his own Use; and now published by Jonathan Edwards, A.M., Minister of the Gospel at Northampton.* See Jonathan Edwards, *The Life of David Brainerd*, Norman Pettit, ed., in *The Works of Jonathan Edwards*, vol. 7 (New Haven, CT: Yale University Press, 1985), p. vii. The reference to Brainerd being thirty years old is inaccurate. He was born April 20, 1718 and died October 9, 1747.

[9] This claim is, of course, hard to substantiate, but others have made even greater claims: "But in truth David Brainerd's life sacrifice reached out and touched the whole world, challenging more people into Christian service than perhaps any other man that ever lived" (Ed Reese, "The Life and Ministry of David Brainerd," *Christian Biography Resources*, http://www.wholesomewords.org/biography/biobrainerd.html [6-1-00]). A more modest claim would be, "Almost immediately upon [the *Diary's*] publication, it captured the hearts of the Protestant world. For over a century it was one of the most popular documents in evangelical circles. Its influence has been enormous" (Francis M. DuBose, ed., *Classics of Christian Missions* [Nashville: Broadman Press, 1979], pp. 173-174).

[10] This summary of his Indian mission is taken from his gravestone in Northampton, MA.

[11] Clyde Kilby, "David Brainerd: Knight of the Grail," *Heroic Colonial Christians*, Russell T. Hitt, ed. (Philadelphia: J. B. Lippincott Company, 1966), p. 202.

With great spiritual privileges comes great pain. It is plain from Scripture that this is God's design: "Because of the surpassing greatness of the revelations," Paul wrote in 2 Corinthians 12:7, "for this reason, to keep me from exalting myself, there was given me a thorn in the flesh, a messenger of Satan to torment me—to keep me from exalting myself!" Great privilege, great pain, God's design. So it was with Bunyan, Cowper, and Brainerd. But they did not all have the same pain. For Bunyan it was prison and danger, for Cowper it was lifelong depression and suicidal darkness, for Brainerd it was tuberculosis and the "howling wilderness."

What was the fruit of this affliction? And what was the rock in which it grew? Consider their stories and be encouraged that no labor and no suffering in the path of Christian obedience is ever in vain. "Behind a frowning providence He hides a smiling face."

ACKNOWLEDGMENTS

After thirty-two years of marriage, she still reads everything I write. She not only reads it, she makes it better. Thank you, Noël, for being my live-in editor.

Justin Taylor took an extra year at Bethlehem Baptist Church on his way through seminary and worked full-time in Desiring God Ministries, helping people think their way through knotty issues in the Bible and theology. Thanks, Justin, for applying your eagle eye to this manuscript as it emerged and for making such helpful suggestions and for catching my bloopers.

Aaron Young does all that a loyal and gifted and intelligent assistant can do to make my life manageable. I would not be able to keep my head above water without his help. Thank you, Aaron, for being there so faithfully behind the scenes, enabling so much.

I love books with indexes that help me find a barely-remembered quote or a forgotten fact. That is why I return again and again to Carol Steinbach to help me make every book more useful with her indexing skills. Thanks, Carol. Now you can read my face when it is time to ask you again.

As with Book One of *The Swans Are Not Silent*, these chapters were originally messages to the Bethlehem Conference for Pastors. It is one of the great joys of my life to encourage brothers in the pastoral ministry by portraying the lives of great saints, and urging them to "consider the outcome of their life, and imitate their faith" (Hebrews 13:7, RSV). These chapters would not exist without the hunger of those pastors to draw out the effort. And the Conference would not exist without Jon Bloom, the director of Desiring God Ministries, and his prayer-filled oversight of this Conference. Thanks, brother, for being there.

Lane Dennis, Ted Griffin, Brian Ondracek, Marvin Padgett, and the whole team at Crossway Books are the indispensable link between writer and reader. Thanks to all of you for caring about the song of the swans and making this project a delight for me.

Finally, God, our Father, and Jesus Christ, our Lord, and the Holy Spirit are to be honored and thanked above all and in all. God is always sufficient for every good work; he is not "served by human hands, as though He needed anything, since He Himself gives to all men life and breath and all things" (Acts 17:25). Sometimes his smile is hidden, but his arm is never shortened, nor his light extinguished. In due season the clouds move, and the light returns, and we are sustained. As we get older we learn to trust the inscrutable working of his winds. May these chapters strengthen you to wait patiently for the Lord in the seasons of darkness, because behind a frowning providence he hides a smiling face.

We also, before the temptation comes, think we can walk upon the

sea, but when the winds blow, we feel ourselves begin to sink. . . .

And yet doth it yield no good unto us? We could not live without

such turnings of the hand of God upon us. We should be

overgrown with flesh, if we had not our seasonable winters.

It is said that in some countries trees will grow,

but will bear no fruit, because there is no winter there.

JOHN BUNYAN

SEASONABLE COUNSEL: OR ADVICE TO SUFFERERS

I saw with the eyes of my soul Jesus Christ at God's right hand;

there, I say, was my righteousness;

so that wherever I was, or whatever I was doing,

God could not say of me, he [lacks] my righteousness,

for that was just before him. . . .

Now did my chains fall off my legs indeed.

I was loosed from my afflictions and irons.

JOHN BUNYAN

GRACE ABOUNDING TO THE CHIEF OF SINNERS

Where the Fruit of Affliction Grows

Three Kinds of Fruit

The afflictions of John Bunyan gave us *The Pilgrim's Progress*. The afflictions of William Cowper gave us "There Is a Fountain Filled with Blood" and "God Moves in a Mysterious Way." And the afflictions of David Brainerd gave us a published *Diary* that has mobilized more missionaries than any other similar work. The furnace of suffering brought forth the gold of guidance and inspiration for living the Christian life, worshiping the Christian God, and spreading the Christian Gospel.

There is a certain irony to the fruit of these afflictions. Bunyan's confinement taught him the pilgrim path of Christian freedom. Cowper's mental illness yielded sweet music of the mind for troubled souls. Brainerd's smoldering misery of isolation and disease exploded in global missions beyond all imagination. Irony and disproportion are all God's way. He keeps us off balance with his unpredictable connections. We think we know how to do something big, and God makes it small. We think that all we have is weak and small, and God makes it big. Barren Sarah gives birth to the child of promise. Gideon's 300 men defeat 100,000 Midianites. A slingshot in the hand of a shepherd boy brings the giant down. A virgin bears the Son of God. A boy's five loaves feed thousands. A breach of justice, groveling political expediency, and criminal torture on a gruesome cross become the foundation of the salvation of the world.

This is God's way—to take all boasting off of man and put it on God. "Not many of you were wise according to worldly standards, not many were powerful, not many were of noble birth; but God chose what is foolish in the world to shame the wise, God chose what is weak in the world to shame the strong, God chose what is low and despised in the world, even things that are not, to bring to nothing things that are, so that no human being might boast in the presence of God. . . . 'Let him who boasts, boast of the Lord'" (1 Corinthians 1:26-29, 31, RSV).

Not surprisingly (1 Peter 4:12), therefore, suffering fits into God's design in ways that sometimes baffle us and test us to the limit. This very baffling and testing is part of the design: "Consider it all joy, my brethren, when you encounter various trials, knowing that the testing of your faith produces endurance. And let endurance have its perfect result, so that you may be perfect and complete, lacking in nothing" (James 1:2-4).

Does God Design Suffering for His Children?

But many stumble at the word *design*. Would suffering be God's design? Can we speak that way? Or should we speak of God working with what he is given? In other words, does God oversee and manage the affairs of the world so that we can speak of suffering as his will and his design, or does he, rather, manage the world like a chess player who does not will the moves of his opponent, but can always check them and turn them for good? Does God plan the place of suffering in the lives of his children for good ends, or is he always in the position of a responder to the pain that other forces give him to work with?

All the swans in this book sing in unison on this question. God governs the world and all that happens in it with purpose and design for the good of those who love him. This was the final lesson Job learned from all his suffering: "Then Job answered the LORD and said, 'I know that You can do all things, and that no purpose of Yours can be thwarted'" (Job 42:1-2). Satan may play his wicked role in the drama and take Job's children and strike him with boils from head to toe, but Job will not give Satan the eminence of ultimate causality. That belongs to God alone, even if we cannot understand it all. When Job's ten children were crushed to death, he "fell upon the ground, and worshiped. And he said, 'Naked I came from my mother's womb, and naked shall I return; the LORD gave, and the LORD has taken away; blessed be the name of the LORD'" (Job 1:20-21, RSV). To this amazing confession that God had taken his children, the author of the book responds with confirmation: "In all this Job did not sin or charge God with wrong" (Job 1:22, RSV). Similarly, even when the text says explicitly that "*Satan* . . . afflicted Job with loathsome sores," Job's response was, "Shall we receive good at the hand of God, and shall we not receive evil?" And again the author endorses Job's theology with the words, "In all this Job did not sin with his lips" (Job 2:7, 10, RSV).

This is the uniform message of the Bible, whether we are talking about suffering that comes from disease[1] or from

---

[1] Exodus 4:11, "The LORD said to him, 'Who has made man's mouth? Or who makes him mute or deaf, or seeing or blind? Is it not I, the LORD?'" John 9:1-3, "[Jesus'] disciples asked Him, 'Rabbi, who sinned, this man or his parents, that he would be born blind?' Jesus answered, 'It was neither that this man sinned, nor his parents; but it was so that the works of God might be displayed in him.'" 2 Samuel 12:15, "Then the LORD struck the child that Uriah's widow bore to David, so that he was very sick." Romans 8:20, "For the creation was subjected to futility, not willingly, but because of Him who subjected it, in hope." See also Job 2:7, 10.

calamity[2] or from persecution[3]: "[God] works all things after the counsel of His will" (Ephesians 1:11). God has a good and wise purpose in all that happens.[4] From morning until night, over all the goings and comings of our lives, we should say, "If the Lord wills, we will live and also do this or that" (James 4:15). Why? Because God says, "My purpose will be established, and I will accomplish all My good pleasure" (Isaiah 46:10). "Many plans are in a man's heart, but the counsel of the LORD will stand" (Proverbs 19:21). "The mind of man plans his way, but the LORD directs his steps" (Proverbs 16:9). "Are not two sparrows sold for a penny? And not one of them will fall to the ground without your Father's will" (Matthew 10:29, RSV). "The king's heart is like channels of water in the hand of the LORD; He turns it wherever He wishes" (Proverbs 21:1). "The lot is cast into the lap, but its every decision is from the LORD" (Proverbs 16:33).

---

[2] Lamentations 3:32-33, 37-38, "For if He causes grief, then He will have compassion according to His abundant lovingkindness. For He does not afflict willingly or grieve the sons of men. . . . Who is there who speaks and it comes to pass, unless the Lord has commanded it? Is it not from the mouth of the Most High that both good and ill go forth?" Amos 3:6, "If a trumpet is blown in a city will not the people tremble? If a calamity occurs in a city has not the LORD done it?" Isaiah 31:2, "Yet He also is wise and will bring disaster." 1 Samuel 2:6-7, "The LORD kills and makes alive; He brings down to Sheol and raises up. The LORD makes poor and rich; He brings low, He also exalts."

[3] Acts 4:27, "For truly in this city there were gathered together against Your holy servant Jesus, whom You anointed, both Herod and Pontius Pilate, along with the Gentiles and the peoples of Israel, to do whatever Your hand and Your purpose predestined to occur." 2 Corinthians 1:8-9, "For we do not want you to be unaware, brethren, of our affliction which came to us in Asia, that we were burdened excessively, beyond our strength, so that we despaired even of life; indeed, we had the sentence of death within ourselves so that we would not trust in ourselves, but in God who raises the dead." 2 Timothy 3:12, "Indeed, all who desire to live godly in Christ Jesus will be persecuted." 1 Peter 2:21, "For you have been called for this purpose, since Christ also suffered for you, leaving you an example for you to follow in His steps." 1 Peter 3:17, "For it is better, if God should will it so, that you suffer for doing what is right rather than for doing what is wrong." 1 Peter 4:19, "Therefore, those also who suffer according to the will of God shall entrust their souls to a faithful Creator in doing what is right." Hebrews 12:4-8, 11, "You have not yet resisted to the point of shedding blood in your striving against sin; and you have forgotten the exhortation which is addressed to you as sons, 'MY SON, DO NOT REGARD LIGHTLY THE DISCIPLINE OF THE LORD, NOR FAINT WHEN YOU ARE REPROVED BY HIM; FOR THOSE WHOM THE LORD LOVES HE DISCIPLINES, AND HE SCOURGES EVERY SON WHOM HE RECEIVES.' It is for discipline that you endure; God deals with you as with sons; for what son is there whom his father does not discipline? But if you

Opposing Voices

Yet there are those will not have it so. There are old-fashioned
liberals who say, "I believe that pain and suffering are never the
will of God for his children. . . . I cannot conceive that it is the
will of God that anyone should be run over by a driver under the
influence of drink, or that a young mother should die of leukemia,
or that some one in the first flush of youth should face the increasing helplessness of arteriosclerosis."[5]

And there are modern-day "open theists"[6] who say, "God

are without discipline, of which all have become partakers, then you are illegitimate children
and not sons. . . . All discipline for the moment seems not to be joyful, but sorrowful; yet to those
who have been trained by it, afterwards it yields the peaceful fruit of righteousness."

[4] For fuller statements of the sovereignty of God in relation to our suffering and how disease
and calamity and persecution are dealt with in Scripture, see John Piper, "Suffering: The Sacrifice
of Christian Hedonism," *Desiring God: Meditations of a Christian Hedonist* (Sisters, OR:
Multnomah Publishers, 1996), pp. 212-238; John Piper, "The Supremacy of God in Missions
Through Suffering," *Let the Nations Be Glad* (Grand Rapids: Baker Book House, 1993), pp.
71-114; John Piper, "The Future Grace of Suffering," in *The Purifying Power of Living by
Faith in Future Grace* (Sisters, OR: Multnomah Publishers, 1995), pp. 341-352.

[5] William Barclay, *A Spiritual Autobiography* (Grand Rapids: William B. Eerdmans Publishing
Co., 1975), p. 44. I call Barclay an "old-fashioned liberal" because his views are similar to
those who summed up Christianity as the fatherhood of God, the brotherhood of man, and
the ethic of love. He was a universalist (pp. 58-60), and the cross of Christ was essentially a
demonstration of God's love, not a substitutionary penal atonement demanded by the righteousness of God (pp. 51-53). With regard to the specifics of doctrine, like Christology, his motto
was: "Hold fast to Christ, and for the rest be totally uncommitted" (p. 97).

[6] *Open theism* is the term chosen by a group of theologians to describe their view that God does
not plan or know all of the future but leaves much of it "open." That is, he does not plan it or
know it ahead of time. Thus, for example, one open theist says, "God is omniscient in the
sense that he knows everything which can be known, just as God is omnipotent in the sense
that he can do everything that can be done. But free actions are not entities which can be
known ahead of time. They literally do not yet exist to be known" (Clark Pinnock, "God
Limits His Knowledge," *Predestination and Free Will: Four Views of Divine Sovereignty and
Freedom* [Downers Grove, IL: InterVarsity Press, 1986], p. 157). Or again he says, "Decisions
not yet made do not exist anywhere to be know even by God" (Pinnock, "From Augustine to
Arminius: A Pilgrimage in Theology," *The Grace of God, The Will of Man: A Case for
Arminianism,* Clark Pinnock, ed. [Grand Rapids: Zondervan Publishing House, 1989], p. 25).
Another open theist puts it like this: "Indeed, to say that God is ignorant of future creaturely
decisions is like saying that God is deaf to silence. It makes no sense, because before they exist
such decisions are nothing for God to be ignorant of" (Richard Rice, "Divine Foreknowledge
and Free-Will Theism," *The Grace of God, The Will of Man,* p. 129). Another says, "In the
Christian view God knows all of reality—everything there is to know. But to assume He knows
ahead of time how every person is going to freely act assumes that each person's free activity is
already there to know—even before he freely does it! But it's not. If we have been given freedom,
we create the reality of our decisions by making them. And until we make them, they don't exist.
Thus, in my view at least, there simply isn't anything to know until we make it there to know.
So God can't foreknow the good or bad decisions of the people He creates until He creates
these people and they, in turn, create their decisions" (Gregory A. Boyd and Edward K. Boyd,
Letters from a Skeptic [Colorado Springs: Chariot Victor Publishing, 1994], p. 30). Other
books representing this viewpoint include *The Openness of God: A Biblical Challenge to the*

does not have a specific divine purpose for each and every occurrence of evil. . . . When a two-month-old child contracts a painful, incurable bone cancer that means suffering and death, it is pointless evil. The Holocaust is pointless evil. The rape and dismemberment of a young girl is pointless evil. The accident that caused the death of my brother was a tragedy. God does not have a specific purpose in mind for these occurrences."[7] "When an individual inflicts pain on another individual, I do not think we can go looking for 'the purpose of God' in the event. . . . I know Christians frequently speak about 'the purpose of God' in the midst of a tragedy caused by someone else. . . . But this I regard to simply be a piously confused way of thinking."[8] "Neither Jesus nor his disciples assumed that there had to be a divine purpose behind all events in history. . . . The Bible does not assume that every particular evil has a particular godly purpose behind it."[9]

"But God Meant It for Good"

And then there is the Bible itself with its resounding claim over every evil perpetrated against God's people: "You meant evil

---

Traditional Understanding of God, Clark Pinnock, ed. (Downers Grove, IL: InterVarsity Press, 1994) and John Sanders, *The God Who Risks: A Theology of Providence* (Downers Grove, IL: InterVarsity Press, 1998). This view has never been embraced as part of orthodoxy by any major Christian body in the history of the church. Thomas Oden, a Wesleyan scholar, along with others, has called it heresy: "If 'reformists' insist on keeping the boundaries of heresy open, however, then they must be resisted with charity. The fantasy that God is ignorant of the future is a heresy that must be rejected on scriptural grounds ('I make known the end from the beginning, from ancient times, what is still to come'; Isa. 46:10a; cf. Job 28; Ps. 90; Rom. 8:29; Eph. 1), as it has been in the history of exegesis of relevant passages. This issue was thoroughly discussed by patristic exegetes as early as Origen's *Against Celsus*" ("The Real Reformers and the Traditionalists," *Christianity Today,* 42 [Feb. 9, 1998], p. 46). For a thorough and compelling critique of open theism, I highly recommend Bruce A. Ware, *God's Lesser Glory: The Diminished God of Open Theism* (Wheaton, IL: Crossway Books, 2000).

[7] Sanders, *The God Who Risks,* p. 262.

[8] Gregory Boyd, *Letters from a Skeptic,* pp. 46-47. In another place he says, "Sickness, disease, war, death, sorrow and tears are not God's will . . ." (*God at War: The Bible and Spiritual Conflict* [Downers Grove, IL: InterVarsity Press, 1997], p. 293).

[9] Boyd, *God at War,* pp. 53, 166.

against me, but God meant it for good in order to bring about this present result, to preserve many people alive" (Genesis 50:20). This is what Joseph said to his brothers who had sinned against him in selling him into slavery and lying to his father Jacob. What he says is not merely that God turned this evil for good after it happened, but that God "meant it" (the same verb as the one used for the brothers' intention) for good. This is confirmed in Genesis 45:7 where Joseph says, "God sent me before you to preserve for you a remnant." In fact, in later centuries the people of Israel celebrated precisely this sovereign design of God in Joseph's trouble, along with the conviction that God planned to bring the famine that made Joseph's presence in Egypt so necessary, and the conviction that God tested Joseph with severe trials:

> *And [God] called for a famine upon the land;*
> *He broke the whole staff of bread.*
> *He sent a man before them,*
> *Joseph, who was sold as a slave.*
> *They afflicted his feet with fetters,*
> *He himself was laid in irons;*
> *Until the time that his word came to pass,*
> *The word of the LORD tested him.*
>
> PSALM 105:16-19

What the Suffering Swans Say

And then there are the swans who suffered. For John Bunyan, William Cowper, and David Brainerd, the loving purpose of God in pain was one of the most precious truths in the Bible and one of the most powerful experiences of their lives. Cowper expressed it in one of his most famous hymns. Notice especially the lines, "He treasures up his bright designs," and "Behind a frowning providence," and "His purposes will ripen fast," and "And scan his work in vain." Each of these lines points to the deep and hope-filled conviction that God has "designs" and "purposes" in his painful "providence" and puzzling "work."

> Deep in unfathomable mines
> Of never-failing skill,
> He treasures up his bright designs
> And works his sovereign will.
>
> Judge not the Lord by feeble sense,
> But trust him for his grace;
> Behind a frowning providence
> He hides a smiling face.
>
> His purposes will ripen fast,
> Unfolding every hour;
> The bud may have a bitter taste,
> But sweet will be the flower.
>
> Blind unbelief is sure to err,
> And scan his work in vain:
> God is his own interpreter,
> And He will make it plain.[10]

David Brainerd shared Cowper's confidence that God governed all that happened to him. This awakened in him what he called a "sweet resignation" in all his extraordinary suffering with

[10] Excerpted from *The Poetical Works of William Cowper*, William Michael Rossetti, ed. (London: William Collins Sons, Ltd.) p. 292.

tuberculosis and loneliness and dangers and all kinds of privations in the wilderness. He wrote in his diary on Sunday, March 10, 1744, "My soul was sweetly resigned to God's disposal of me, in every regard; and I saw there had nothing happened to me but what was best for me."[11] Even the disappointments of ministering in a "dry and barren" spiritual condition he saw within the designs of his Father's care:

> It pleased God to leave me to be very dry and barren; so that I don't remember to have been so straightened for a whole twelve month past. God is just, and he has made my soul acquiesce in his will in this regard. 'Tis contrary to "flesh and blood" to be cut off from all freedom in a large auditory [audience], where their expectations are much raised; but so it was with me: and God helped me to say "Amen" to it; good is the will of the Lord.[12]

If anyone should begin to wonder if such submission to the sovereign will of God over all things would produce a passive fatalism, all one has to do is look honestly at Brainerd's life. It produced the opposite. He was empowered to press on against immense obstacles with the confidence that God was working for him in every trial. "This, through grace, I can say at present, with regard to the life or death: 'The Lord do with me as seems good in his sight.'"[13]

The Old Testament context for that last quote confirms the empowering and freeing effect of believing in God's triumphant

---

[11] Jonathan Edwards, *The Life of David Brainerd*, Norman Pettit, ed., *The Works of Jonathan Edwards*, vol. 7 (New Haven, CT: Yale University Press, 1985), p. 242.

[12] Ibid., p. 316. A diary entry dated Lord's Day, August 18, 1745.

[13] Ibid., p. 431. A diary entry dated Tuesday, September 30, 1746.

sovereignty over the battles of life. Joab and his brother Abishai, with the army of Israel, were arrayed against the Syrians and the Ammonites. The outcome looked precarious. So Joab said to his brother, "If the Syrians are too strong for me, then you shall help me; but if the Ammonites are too strong for you, then I will help you. Be of good courage, and let us play the man for our people, and for the cities of our God; and may the LORD do what seems good to him" (1 Chronicles 19:12-13, RSV). The Lord was in control of the outcome. But this did not paralyze Joab with fatalism; it empowered with hope. Come what may—defeat or victory—the Lord is in control and has his "bright designs." Even if the bloody "bud" of battle turns out to have a bitter taste, "sweet" will be the "flower" of God's design.

Bunyan's Counsel for Those Who Suffer

John Bunyan wrote more on suffering and the fruitfulness of affliction than Cowper or Brainerd. He was even more explicit that there is divine purpose and design in suffering for the good of God's children and for the glory of his name. The great *Pilgrim's Progress*, as George Whitefield said, "smells of the prison." It was born in suffering, and it portrays the Christian life as a life of affliction. But Bunyan saw his imprisonment as no more than what God had designed for him: "So being delivered up to the jailer's hand, I was had home to prison, and there have lain now complete for twelve years, waiting to see what God would suffer those men to do with me."[14]

---

[14] John Bunyan, *Grace Abounding to the Chief of Sinners* (Hertfordshire: Evangelical Press, 1978), p. 20.

The richest source of teaching on suffering in the writings of Bunyan is a book that he wrote for his own congregation titled *Seasonable Counsel, or Advice to Sufferers*.[15] It appeared in 1684 just before the "Bloody Assizes."[16] The need for this "seasonable counsel" was not theoretical. Some of his parishioners had already been imprisoned with him. The threat was so real again that Bunyan deeded over all his possessions to his wife Elizabeth in the expectation that he might be imprisoned and made to pay fines that would take all his possessions.[17] It was no exaggeration when Bunyan wrote, "Our days indeed have been days of trouble, especially since the discovery of the Popish plot, for then we began to fear cutting of throats, of being burned in our beds, and of seeing our children dashed in pieces before our faces."[18]

What, then, would he say to his people to prepare them for the probability of their suffering for Christ? Would he say, with the old-fashioned liberal, "I believe that pain and suffering are never the will of God for his children"? Would he say with the modern-day open theist, "Christians frequently speak about 'the purpose of God' in the midst of a tragedy caused by someone else. . . . But this I regard to simply be a piously confused way of thinking"? No, this would have been biblically and pastorally unthinkable for John Bunyan, whose blood was "bibline."[19]

He takes his text from 1 Peter 4:19, "Wherefore let them that suffer according to the will of God commit the keeping of their

[15] John Bunyan, *Seasonable Counsel, or Advice to Sufferers*, in *The Works of John Bunyan*, vol. 2, George Offor, ed. (Edinburgh: The Banner of Truth Trust, 1991), pp. 691-741.
[16] See Chapter One, note 12.
[17] John Brown, *John Bunyan: His Life, Times and Work* (London: The Hulbert Publishing Company, 1928), p. 338.
[18] John Bunyan, *Israel's Hope Encouraged*, in *The Works of John Bunyan*, vol. 1, p. 585.
[19] Charles Spurgeon, *Autobiography*, vol. 2 (Edinburgh: The Banner of Truth Trust, 1973), p. 159.

soul to him in well doing, as unto a faithful Creator" (KJV). Then he explains the text with these observations:

> It is not what enemies will, nor what they are resolved upon, but what God will, and what God appoints, that shall be done. . . . And as no enemy can bring suffering upon a man when the will of God is otherwise, so no man can save himself out of their hands when God will deliver him up for his glory. . . . We shall or shall not suffer, even as it pleaseth him. . . . God has appointed who shall suffer. Suffering comes not by chance or by the will of man, but by the will and appointment of God.[20]

He goes on to say that God has appointed not only who shall suffer but also when, where, in what way, for how long, and for what truth they shall suffer.[21]

"God's Hook Is in Their Nose"

Whether there have been serious and loving pastors in the history of the church who during times of great persecution have pointed their people to a God who has no control over and no purpose in their suffering, I do not know. But such counsel would have been viewed as untrue and unloving by Bunyan, Cowper, and Brainerd. They knew another God, and they lived with a different confidence. Bunyan summed up the involvement of God in the persecutions of his people like this:

All the ways of the persecutors are God's. Daniel 5:23.

---

[20] Bunyan, *Seasonable Counsel, or Advice to Sufferers*, pp. 722-723.
[21] See Chapter One for the details of his argument and the texts he gives to support them.

Wherefore, as we should, so again we should not, be afraid of men: we should be afraid of them, because they will hurt us; but we should not be afraid of them, as if they were let loose to do to us, and with us, what they will. God's bridle is upon them, God's hook is in their nose: yea, and God has determined the bounds of their rage, and if he lets them drive his church into the sea of troubles, it shall be but up to the neck, and so far it may go, and not be drowned. 2 Kings 19:28; Isaiah 37:29; 8:7-8. I say the Lord has hold of them, and orders them; nor do they at any time come out against his people but by his license and compassion how far to go, and where to stop.[22]

This robust view of God's rule over his enemies is the foundation of Bunyan's consolation as he ministers to his people:

I have, in a few words, handled this . . . to show you that our sufferings are ordered and disposed by him, that you might always, when you come into trouble for this name, not stagger nor be at loss, but be stayed, composed, and settled in your minds, and say, 'The will of the Lord be done.' Acts 21:14 . . . How kindly, therefore, doth God deal with us, when he chooses to afflict us but for a little, that with everlasting kindness he may have mercy upon us. Isaiah 54:7-8.[23]

"My Father's Wise Bestowment"

This is the vision of God's sovereign and mysterious kindness that has sustained Christians in every century and from all parts of the world. It is the vision that underlies scores of hymns that the

---

[22] Bunyan, *Seasonable Counsel, or Advice to Sufferers*, pp. 725-726.
[23] Ibid., pp. 724, 737.

people of God have sung through many storms. Indeed, the great hymns usually come from the experience of suffering and prove by their existence the truth of their message—that afflictions bear fruit for the people of God. Examples come not only from William Cowper, but from others as well.

Karolina Wilhelmina Sandell-Berg (Lina Sandell) "was the daughter of Jonas Sandell, pastor of the Lutheran church in Fröderyd, Sweden. At age twenty-six, she accompanied her father on a boat trip to Gothenberg, during which he fell overboard and drowned before her eyes. The tragedy profoundly affected Lina and inspired her to write hymns,"[24] one of the best known of which is "Day by Day."

> Day by day, and with each passing moment,
> Strength I find, to meet my trials here;
> Trusting in my Father's wise bestowment,
> I've no cause for worry or for fear.
> He Whose heart is kind beyond all measure
> Gives unto each day what He deems best—
> Lovingly, its part of pain and pleasure,
> Mingling toil with peace and rest.

This is the same vision of God's sovereign kindness that we saw in Bunyan's *Seasonable Counsel.* Our God is "kind beyond all measure." What he gives is a "Father's wise bestowment," which means he gives to each day "what He deems best—lovingly, its part of *pain* and pleasure." This wisely and lovingly apportioned pain gives us "strength to meet [our] trials here." The truth and beauty

---

[24] "Karolina Wilhelmina Sandell-Berg," *The Cyber Hymnal,* http://tch.simplenet.com/bio/s/a/sandell-berg_kw.htm (6-2-00).

of this hymn was the fruit of affliction and goes on helping us "consider it all joy" (James 1:2) so that the affliction of our own lives may yield "the peaceful fruit of righteousness" (Hebrews 12:11).

Baptist, Anglican, Congregationalist: All Justified Through Faith

The suffering of persecution was not bestowed equally to John Bunyan, William Cowper, and David Brainerd. But there was another form of affliction that brings these three together, and the remedy for it was cherished by them all, even though it bore fruit very differently in their lives. The affliction was the terrifying mental turmoil and darkness of guilt before God, and the remedy for it was the great biblical truth of justification by grace through faith alone. Bunyan was a Baptist, Cowper an Anglican, and Brainerd a Congregationalist. One of the great mercies of God is that, in their times, the doctrine of justification was clear and common to all of them.

"Now Did My Chains Fall off My Legs Indeed"

The *Second London Confession* was forged by Baptists in Bunyan's lifetime and published in its final form in 1689, the year after he died. Built on the *Westminster Confession of Faith*, it was crystal-clear on justification.

> Those whom God effectually calleth He also freely justifieth; not by infusing righteousness into them, but by pardoning their sins, and by accounting and accepting their

persons as righteous; not for anything wrought in them, or done by them, but for Christ's sake alone, not by imputing faith itself, the act of believing, or any other evangelical obedience, to them as their righteousness; but by imputing Christ's active obedience unto the whole law, and passive obedience in his death for their whole and sole righteousness, receiving and resting on Him, and His righteousness, by faith; which faith they have not of themselves, it is the gift of God.

Faith, thus receiving and resting on Christ and His righteousness, is the alone instrument of justification; yet is it not alone in the person justified, but is ever accompanied with all other saving graces, and is no dead faith, but worketh by love.[25]

This was the truth that rescued Bunyan from the terrors of feeling hopelessly damned. "Oh, no one knows the terrors of those days but myself."[26] Then comes what seemed to be the decisive moment.

One day as I was passing into the field . . . this sentence fell upon my soul. Thy righteousness is in heaven. And methought, withal, I saw with the eyes of my soul Jesus Christ at God's right hand; there, I say, was my righteousness; so that wherever I was, or whatever I was doing, God could not say of me, he wants [lacks] my righteousness, for that was just before him. I also saw, moreover, that it was not my good frame of heart that made my righteousness better, nor yet my bad frame that made my righteousness worse, for my righteousness was Jesus Christ himself,

[25] *The Second London Confession*, 1677 and 1689, Chapter 11:1-2, quoted in *John A. Broadus: Baptist Confessions, Covenants, and Catechisms*, Timothy and Denise George, eds. (Nashville: Broadman & Holman Publishers, 1996), pp. 69-70.

[26] *Grace Abounding*, p. 59.

"The same yesterday, today, and forever." Hebrews 13:8.
Now did my chains fall off my legs indeed. I was loosed
from my afflictions and irons. . . . Now went I also home
rejoicing for the grace and love of God.[27]

"I Think I Should Have Died with Gratitude and Joy"

The solid foundation of *The Thirty-Nine Articles of Religion of
the Church of England* (framed in 1571) had been around for
almost 150 years when William Cowper, the Anglican, experienced the power of its truth on justification. Article 11, "Of the
Justification of Man," says,

We are accounted righteous before God, only for the merit
of our Lord and Savior Jesus Christ by Faith, and not of
our own works or deservings. Wherefore, that we are justified by Faith only, is a most wholesome Doctrine, and
very full of comfort. . . .[28]

Comfort indeed to the young Cowper who had been committed to an insane asylum for his suicidal depression. There a man
of God applied to him the truths of the Gospel again and again.
Slowly Cowper began to feel some hope. One day he opened the
Bible at random, and the first verse he saw was Romans 3:25,
"Whom God hath set forth to be a propitiation through faith in his
blood, to declare his righteousness for the remission of sins that are
past, through the forbearance of God" (KJV). He marks his conversion from this moment, because, as he says,

---

[27] Ibid., pp. 90-91.
[28] Quoted from *Creeds of Christendom,* vol. 3, Philip Schaff, ed. (Grand Rapids: Baker Book House, 1977), p. 494, citing the American Revision of 1801.

Immediately I received the strength to believe it, and the full beams of the Sun of Righteousness shone upon me. I saw the sufficiency of the atonement He had made, my pardon sealed in His blood, and all the fullness and completeness of His justification. In a moment I believed, and received the gospel. . . . Unless the Almighty arm had been under me, I think I should have died with gratitude and joy. My eyes filled with tears, and my voice choked with transport; I could only look up to heaven in silent fear, overwhelmed with love and wonder.[29]

Again it is "the completeness of [Christ's] justification" that the Holy Spirit used to awaken and rescue Cowper from the darkness of damnation that had settled over him. The war for Cowper's soul was not ended, but the decisive battle had been fought and won by the Gospel of justification by grace through faith.

"This Way of Salvation, Entirely by the Righteousness of Christ"

The *Westminster Shorter Catechism* formed the doctrinal foundation of life and ministry for David Brainerd, the Congregationalist (with Presbyterian leanings[30]). He used it among his Indian converts,[31] as he had grown up on it himself. Question 33 asks, "What is Justification?" and answers, "Justification is an act of God's free grace, wherein he pardoneth all our sins, and accepteth us as

---

[29] Gilbert Thomas, *William Cowper and the Eighteenth Century* (London: Ivor Nicholson and Watson, Ltd., 1935), p. 132.

[30] Edwards, *The Life of David Brainerd*, p. 58.

[31] Ibid., p. 345.

righteous in his sight, only for the righteousness of Christ imputed to us, and received by faith alone."[32]

On the Lord's Day, July 12, 1739, at the age of twenty-one, Brainerd experienced a conversion that marked the rest of his life.

> At this time, the way of salvation opened to me with such infinite wisdom, suitableness, and excellency, that I wondered I should ever think of any other way of salvation; was amazed I had not dropped my own contrivances, and complied with this lovely, blessed, and excellent way before. If I could have been saved by my own duties, or any other way that I had formerly contrived, my whole soul would [now] have refused it. I wondered [that] all the world did not see and comply with this way of salvation, entirely by the righteousness of Christ.[33]

As with Bunyan and Cowper, it is the "way of salvation, entirely by the righteousness of Christ," that breaks through the darkness of doubt and unbelief and wakens new life.

And not just at the beginning of his walk with God, but also at the end of his life, this is the truth that sustained him. On Saturday, September 19, 1747, less than three weeks before he died, he wrote about how God sustained him in a moment of self-recrimination:

> Near night, while I attempted to walk a little, my thoughts turned thus, "How infinitely sweet it is to love God and be all for Him!" Upon which it was suggested to me, "You are not an angel, not lively and active." To which my whole soul immediately replied, "I as sincerely desire to love and

---

[32] Quoted from *Creeds of Christendom*, vol. 3, Schaff, ed. (Grand Rapids: Baker Book House, 1977), p. 683.

[33] Edwards, *The Life of David Brainerd*, p. 140.

glorify God, as any angel in heaven." Upon which it was suggested again, "But you are filthy, not fit for heaven." Hereupon instantly appeared the blessed robes of Christ's righteousness which I could not but exult and triumph in.[34]

Where the Fruit of Affliction Grows

Is it not remarkable that the song of these three suffering swans should be so similar at the crucial moments of their conversions? The righteousness of Christ, outside themselves, imputed to them through faith alone, did not make wastrels of them but worshipers. It did not lead them into profligate living but impelled them into the pursuit of holiness. It did not leave them self-satisfied but set them to preaching and writing and evangelizing. It sustained them through all suffering (for Cowper, barely—1 Peter 4:18) and formed the solid ground where the fruit of affliction could grow and the tree not be broken.

Under God's sovereign grace, then, what we have to thank for the great allegory of Bunyan and the hymns of Cowper and the life of Brainerd is, first, the glorious biblical truth of Christ's righteousness imputed by grace through faith alone, and second, the merciful gift of affliction. We are the beneficiaries today of the fruit of their affliction. And God's design in it is that we not lose heart, but trust him that someone also will be strengthened by the fruit of ours. Behind a frowning providence he hides a smiling face. We may see it in our lifetime, or we may not. But the whole Bible is written, and all the swans are singing, to convince us it is there, and that we can and should "exult in our tribulations" (Romans 5:3).

---

[34] Ibid., p. 465.

I was made to see that if ever I would suffer rightly,

I must first pass a sentence of death upon everything

that can be properly called a thing of this life,

even to reckon myself, my wife, my children,

my health, my enjoyment, and all, as dead to me,

and myself as dead to them.

The second was, to live upon God that is invisible.

JOHN BUNYAN
GRACE ABOUNDING TO THE CHIEF OF SINNERS

1

"To Live upon God That Is Invisible"

Suffering and Service in the Life of John Bunyan

"Bless You, Prison, for Having Been in My Life!"

In 1672, about fifty miles northwest of London in Bedford, John Bunyan was released from twelve years of imprisonment. As with suffering saints before and since, Bunyan found prison to be a painful and fruitful gift. He would have understood the words of Aleksandr Solzhenitsyn, 300 years later, who, like Bunyan, turned his imprisonment into a world-changing work of explosive art. After his imprisonment in the Russian gulag of Joseph Stalin's "corrective labor camps," Solzhenitsyn wrote:

> It was granted to me to carry away from my prison years on my bent back, which nearly broke beneath its load, this essential experience: how a human being becomes evil and how good. In the intoxication of youthful successes I had felt myself to be infallible, and I was therefore cruel. In the surfeit of power I was a murderer and an oppressor. In my most evil moments I was convinced that I was doing good, and I was well supplied with systematic arguments. It was only when I lay there on rotting prison straw that I sensed within myself the first stirrings of good. Gradually it was disclosed to me that

the line separating good and evil passes not through states, nor between classes, nor between political parties either— but right through every human heart—and through all human hearts. . . . That is why I turn back to the years of my imprisonment and say, sometimes to the astonishment of those about me: *"Bless you, prison!"* I . . . have served enough time there. I nourished my soul there, and I say without hesitation: *"Bless you, prison*, for having been in my life!"* [1]

How can a man pronounce a blessing on imprisonment? Bunyan's life and labor give one answer. Just before his release (it seems[2]), at age forty-four, Bunyan updated his spiritual auto-biography called *Grace Abounding to the Chief of Sinners*. He looked back over the hardships of the last twelve years and wrote about how he was enabled by God to survive and even flourish in the Bedford jail. One of his comments gives me the title for this chapter.

He quotes from the New Testament where the apostle Paul says, "We had the sentence of death within ourselves so that we would not trust in ourselves, but in God who raises the dead" (2 Corinthians 1:9). Then he says,

> By this scripture I was made to see that if ever I would suffer rightly, I must *first* pass a sentence of death upon everything that can be properly called a thing of this life, even to reckon myself, my wife, my children, my health,

---

[1] Aleksandr I. Solzhenitsyn, *The Gulag Archipelago: 1918-1956. An Experiment in Literary Investigation*, Thomas P. Whitney, trans., vol. 2 (New York: HarperCollins, 1975; Boulder: Westview Press, 1997), pp. 615-617.

[2] According to Bunyan's *Grace Abounding to the Chief of Sinners* (Hertfordshire, England: Evangelical Press, 1978), p. 109, the first part of this "autobiography" was written after Bunyan had been in prison for about five years. But on p. 120 he says, "I . . . have lain now complete for twelve years, waiting to see what God would suffer those men to do with me."

my enjoyment, and all, as dead to me, and myself as dead to them. The *second* was, *to live upon God that is invisible*, as Paul said in another place; the way not to faint, is to "look not at the things which are seen, but at the things which are not seen; for the things which are seen are temporal, but the things which are not seen are eternal."[3]

I have not found any phrase in Bunyan's writings that captures better the key to his life than this one: "To live upon God that is invisible." He learned that if we are to suffer well, we must die not only to sin, but also to the imperious claims of precious and innocent things, including family and freedom. While in prison he confessed concerning his wife and children, "I am somewhat too fond of these great Mercies."[4] Thus we must learn to "live upon God that is invisible," not only because God is superior to sinful pleasures, but also because he is superior to sacred ones as well. Everything else in the world we must count as dead to us and we to it.

He learned this from prison and he learned from Paul: "Far be it from me to glory except in the cross of our Lord Jesus Christ, by which the world has been crucified to me, and I to the world" (Galatians 6:14, RSV). Death to the world was the costly corollary of life to God. The visible world died to Bunyan. He lived on "God that is invisible." Increasingly this was Bunyan's passion from the time of his conversion as a young married man to the day of his death when he was sixty years old.

---

[3] Ibid., p. 122 (emphasis added).
[4] Ibid., p. 123.

Suffering: Normal and Essential

In all my reading of Bunyan, what has gripped me most is his suffering and how he responded to it, what it made of him, and what it might make of us. All of us come to our tasks with a history and many predispositions. I come to John Bunyan with a growing sense that suffering is a normal and useful and essential element in Christian life and ministry. It not only weans us off the world and teaches us to live on God, as 2 Corinthians 1:9 says, but also makes ministers more able to strengthen the church[5] and makes missionaries more able to reach the nations[6] with the Gospel of the grace of God.

I am influenced in the way I read Bunyan both by what I see in the world today and what I see in the Bible. As you read this page, the flashpoints of suffering will have changed since I wrote it. But the reality will not—not as long as the world stays and the Word of Jesus stands. "In the world you have tribulation" (John 16:33). "Behold, I send you out as sheep in the midst of wolves" (Matthew 10:16). Today churches are being burned in some countries, and Christian young people are being killed by anti-Christian mobs. Christians endure systematic starvation and enslavement. China perpetuates its official repression of religious freedom and lengthy imprisonments. India, with its one billion people and unparalleled diversity, heaves with tensions between major religions and with

---

[5] "Therefore I endure everything for the sake of the elect, that they also may obtain salvation in Christ Jesus with its eternal glory" (2 Timothy 2:10, RSV). "I rejoice in my sufferings for your sake, and in my flesh I complete what is lacking in Christ's afflictions for the sake of his body, that is, the church" (Colossians 1:24, RSV).

[6] "Behold, I send you out as sheep in the midst of wolves; so be shrewd as serpents and innocent as doves. But beware of men, for they will hand you over to the courts and scourge you in their synagogues; and *you will even be brought before governors and kings for My sake, as a testimony to them and to the Gentiles* [nations]" (Matthew 10:16-18, emphasis added). "Those who were scattered *because of the persecution* that occurred in connection with Stephen made their way to Phoenicia and Cyprus and Antioch, speaking the word. . . . Some of them . . . began speaking to the Greeks also, preaching the Lord Jesus" (Acts 11:19-20, emphasis added).

occasional violence. The estimate of how many Christians are martyred each year surpasses all ability to weep as we ought.[7]

As I write, I see thousands dead in the paths of hurricanes or killed by earthquakes. I see hundreds slaughtered in war. I see thirty-three million people worldwide infected with HIV, the virus that causes AIDS. Almost six million new people are infected with the virus each year (eleven people every minute). "By the end of [2000], there will be ten million AIDS orphans."[8] More than 6,000 people are dying every day from AIDS. And, of course, I see the people suffering in my own church with tuberculosis and lupus and heart disease and blindness, not to mention the hundreds of emotional and relational pangs that people would trade any day for a good clean amputation.

And as I come to Bunyan's life and suffering, I see in the Bible that "through many tribulations we must enter the kingdom" (Acts 14:22); and the promise of Jesus, "If they persecuted Me, they will also persecute you" (John 15:20); and the warning from Peter "not [to] be surprised at the fiery ordeal among you, which comes upon you for your testing, as though some strange thing were happening to you" (1 Peter 4:12); and the utter realism of Paul that we who have "the first fruits of the Spirit, even we ourselves groan within ourselves, waiting eagerly for our adoption as sons, the redemption of our body" (Romans 8:23); and the reminder that "our outer nature is wasting away" (2 Corinthians 4:16, RSV), and that the whole creation "was subjected to futility" (Romans 8:20).

As I look around me in the world and in the Word of God,

[7] David Barrett and Todd M. Johnson, "Annual Statistical Table on Global Mission: 1999," vol. 23, no. 1, *International Bulletin of Missionary Research*, p. 25, estimated 164,000 Christian martyrs in 1999.

[8] *StarTribune*, Minneapolis, May 13, 2000, p. A19.

my own sense is that what we need from Bunyan is a glimpse into how he suffered and how he learned "to live upon God that is invisible." I want that for myself and my family and the church I serve and for all who read this book. For nothing glorifies God more than maintaining our stability and joy when we lose everything but God. That day is coming for each of us, and we do well to get ready, and to help the people we love get ready.

The Times of the Redwoods

John Bunyan was born in Elstow, about a mile south of Bedford, England, in 1628, the same year that William Laud became the bishop of London during the reign of King Charles I. The connection with Bishop Laud is important because we can't understand the sufferings of Bunyan apart from the religious and political times in which he lived.

In those days there were tremendous conflicts between Parliament and monarchy. Bishop Laud, together with Charles I, opposed the reforms of the Church of England desired by the Puritans—those pastors and teachers between 1550 and 1700 who longed to see the Church of England "purified" with biblical truth and fire, and whom J. I. Packer calls the California Redwoods in the forest of Christianity.[9] Both Laud and King

---

[9] "California's redwoods make me think of England's Puritans, another breed of giants who in our time have begun to be newly appreciated. Between 1550 and 1700 they too lived unfrilled lives in which, speaking spiritually, strong growth and resistance to fire and storm were what counted. As redwoods attract the eye, because they overtop other trees, so the mature holiness and seasoned fortitude of the great Puritans shine before us as a kind of beacon light, overtopping the stature of the majority of Christians in most eras, and certainly so in this age of crushing urban collectivism, when Western Christians sometimes feel and often look like ants in an anthill and puppets on a string" (J. I. Packer, *A Quest for Godliness: The Puritan Vision of the Christian Life* [Wheaton, IL: Crossway Books, 1990], pp. 11-12). This book is an excellent, readable introduction to the life and thought of that generation of Christian giants.

Charles pressed to bring all the Church of England into High Church conformity along the lines of the *Book of Common Prayer*—against the consciences of many Puritans.

Oliver Cromwell—a Puritan champion in the political realm—was elected to Parliament in 1640, and civil war broke out in 1642 between the forces loyal to the king and those loyal to Parliament—and to the reforms that Puritans longed for. In 1645, the Parliament took control of the monarchy. Bishop Laud was executed that year on January 10, and the mandatory use of the *Book of Common Prayer* was overthrown. The Westminster Assembly completed the *Westminster Confession* for the dominant Presbyterian church in 1646. The king, Charles I, was beheaded in 1649, and his son, Charles II, escaped to the continent. Cromwell led the new Commonwealth until his death in 1658. His main concern was a stable government with freedom of religion for Puritans like John Bunyan and others. "Jews, who had been excluded from England since 1290, were allowed to return in 1655."[10]

After Cromwell's death, his son Richard was unable to hold the government together. The longing for stability with a new king swelled. How quickly the favor of man can turn! The Parliament turned against the nonconformists like John Bunyan and passed a series of acts that resulted in increased restrictions on the Puritan preachers. Charles II was brought home in what is known as the Restoration of the Monarchy and was proclaimed king in 1660, the same year that Bunyan was imprisoned for preaching without state approval.

---

[10] "Cromwell, Oliver," *Microsoft® Encarta® 98 Encyclopedia.* © 1993-1997 Microsoft Corporation. All rights reserved.

Two Thousand Pastors Ejected

In 1662, the Act of Uniformity was passed that required accep-
tance, again, of the *Book of Common Prayer* and Episcopal
ordination. That August, two thousand Puritan pastors were
forced out of their churches. Twelve years later there was a
happy turn of affairs with the "Declaration of Religious
Indulgence" that resulted in Bunyan's freedom, his license to
preach, and his call as the official pastor of the nonconformist
church in Bedford. But there was political instability until he
died in 1688 at the age of sixty. He was imprisoned one other
time in the mid-1670s, during which he wrote *The Pilgrim's
Progress.*[11]

These were the days of John Bunyan's sufferings, and we
must be careful not to overstate or understate the terror of the
days. We would overstate it if we thought he was tortured in the
Bedford jail. In fact, some jailers let him out to see his family or
make brief trips. But we would understate it if we thought he
was not in frequent danger of execution. For example, in the
Bloody Assizes[12] of 1685, more than three hundred people were
put to death in the western counties of England for doing no
more than Bunyan did as a nonconformist pastor.

[11] Scholars differ about the time *The Pilgrim's Progress* was actually written. Some conclude that
it was during the first imprisonment of 1660-1672 (Barry Horner, *The Pilgrim's Progress* [North
Brunswick, NJ: n.p., 1997], p. xvii), and some that it was written during the second imprisonment of 1675 (John Brown, *John Bunyan: His Life, Times, and Work* [London: The Hulbert
Publishing Co., 1928], p. 174). We do know that it was finally published for the first time in
1678.

[12] "Bloody Assizes" refers "in English history [to] the trials conducted in the west of England
by the chief justice, George Jeffreys, 1st Baron Jeffreys of Wem, and four other judges after the
abortive rebellion (June 1685) of the Duke of Monmouth, illegitimate son of King Charles II,
against his Roman Catholic uncle King James II. About 320 persons were hanged and more than
800 transported to Barbados; hundreds more were fined, flogged, or imprisoned." "Bloody
Assizes," *Encyclopedia Britannica,* http://www.britannica.com/bcom/eb/article/idxref/5/
0,5716,483175,00.html (5-25-00).

Young Heartache and Fear

Bunyan learned the trade of metalworking or "tinker" or "brasyer"[13] from his father. He received the ordinary education of the poor to read and write, but nothing more. He had no formal higher education of any kind, which makes his writing and influence all the more astonishing. The more notable suffering of his life began in his teens. In 1644, when he was fifteen, his mother and sister died within one month of each other. His sister was thirteen. To add to the heartache, his father remarried within a month. All this while not many miles away, in that same month of loss, the king attacked a church in Leighton and "began to cut and wound right and left."[14] And later that fall, when Bunyan had turned sixteen, he was drafted into the Parliamentary Army and for about two years was taken from his home for military service. There were harrowing moments, he recounts, as for example once when a man took his place as a sentinel and was shot in the head with a musket ball and died.[15]

Bunyan was not a Christian believer during this time. He tells us, "I had few equals, especially considering my years . . . for cursing, swearing, lying, and blaspheming the holy name of God. . . . Until I came to the state of marriage, I was the very ringleader of all the youth that kept me company, in all manner of vice and ungodliness."[16]

---

[13] This is the term he uses to describe his occupation in his own will. John Brown, *John Bunyan*, p. 29. It refers to repairing tools with hammer and forge.

[14] Ibid., p. 42.

[15] Ibid., p. 45.

[16] John Bunyan, *Grace Abounding*, pp. 10-11.

Precious Books Came with His Wife

He "came to the state of matrimony" when he was twenty or twenty-one, but we never learn his wife's name. What we do learn is that she was poor, but had a godly father who had died and left her two books that she brought to the marriage, *The Plain Man's Pathway to Heaven* and *The Practice of Piety*.[17] Bunyan said, "In these two books I would sometimes read with her, wherein I also found some things that were somewhat pleasing to me; but all this while I met with no conviction."[18] But God's work had begun. He was irreversibly drawing the young married Bunyan to himself.

John and his wife had four children: Mary, Elizabeth, John, and Thomas. Mary, the oldest, was born blind. This not only added to the tremendous burden of his heart in caring for Mary and the others, but it would also make his imprisonment, when Mary was ten years old, an agonizing separation.[19]

"Thy Righteousness Is in Heaven"

During the first five years of marriage, Bunyan was profoundly converted to Christ and to the baptistic, nonconformist church life in Bedford. He came under the influence of John Gifford, the pastor in Bedford, and moved from Elstow to Bedford with his family and joined the church there in 1653, though he was not as sure as they were that he was a Christian. Pastor Gifford, he

---

[17] Both of these books have been made available in recent years: Arthur Dent, *The Plain Man's Pathway to Heaven* (Morgan, PA: Soli Deo Gloria, 1997), and Lewis Bayly, *The Practice of Piety* (Morgan, PA: Soli Deo Gloria, 1994).

[18] *Grace Abounding*, p. 13.

[19] See below p. 56.

wrote, was willing to think him a Christian, "though, I think, from little grounds."[20] It's hard to put a date on his conversion because in retelling the process in *Grace Abounding to the Chief of Sinners* he includes almost no dates or times. But it was a lengthy and agonizing process.

He was poring over the Scriptures but finding no peace or assurance. There were seasons of great doubt about the Scriptures and about his own soul. "A whole flood of blasphemies, both against God, Christ, and the Scriptures were poured upon my spirit, to my great confusion and astonishment. . . . How can you tell but that the Turks had as good scriptures to prove their Mahomet the Savior as we have to prove our Jesus?"[21] "My heart was at times exceeding hard. If I would have given a thousand pounds for a tear, I could not shed one."[22]

When he thought that he was established in the Gospel, there came a season of overwhelming darkness following a terrible temptation when he heard the words, "sell and part with this most blessed Christ. . . . Let him go if he will." He tells us that "I felt my heart freely consent thereto. Oh, the diligence of Satan; oh, the desperateness of man's heart."[23] For two years, he tells us, he was in the doom of damnation. "I feared that this wicked sin of mine might be that sin unpardonable."[24] "Oh, no one knows the terrors of those days but myself."[25] "I found it a hard work now to pray to God because despair was swallowing me up."[26]

---

[20] *Grace Abounding*, p. 33.
[21] Ibid., p. 40.
[22] Ibid., p. 43.
[23] Ibid., pp. 54-55.
[24] Ibid., p. 57.
[25] Ibid., p. 59.
[26] Ibid., p. 63.

Then comes what seemed to be the decisive moment.

One day as I was passing into the field . . . this sentence
fell upon my soul. Thy righteousness is in heaven. And
methought, withal, I saw with the eyes of my soul Jesus
Christ at God's right hand; there, I say, was my righteousness; so that wherever I was, or whatever I was doing, God
could not say of me, he wants [lacks] my righteousness,
for that was just before him. I also saw, moreover, that it
was not my good frame of heart that made my righteousness better, nor yet my bad frame that made my righteousness worse, for my righteousness was Jesus Christ himself,
"The same yesterday, today, and forever." Hebrews 13:8.
Now did my chains fall off my legs indeed. I was loosed
from my afflictions and irons; my temptations also fled
away; so that from that time those dreadful scriptures of
God [about the unforgivable sin] left off to trouble me; now
went I also home rejoicing for the grace and love of God.[27]

It is no accident that this echoes the story of Martin Luther's
conversion.[28] Under God, one key influence here, besides Pastor
Gifford in Bedford, was Martin Luther. "The God in whose hands

---

[27] Ibid., pp. 90-91.
[28] Luther, like Bunyan, agonized in the fear that God's righteousness meant his condemnation. For both of them the precious teaching of the Scripture on justification by faith alone was the light that broke through the darkness of their hopelessness. Luther wrote about it like this: "At last, by the mercy of God, meditating day and night, I gave heed to the context of the words [Romans 1:16-17], namely, 'In it the righteousness of God is revealed, as it is written, "He who through faith is righteous shall live."' There I began to understand [that] the righteous-ness of God is that by which the righteous lives by a gift of God, namely by faith. And this is the meaning: the righteousness of God is revealed by the gospel, namely, the passive righteous-ness with which [the] merciful God justifies us by faith, as it is written, 'He who through faith is righteous shall live.' Here I felt that I was altogether born again and had entered paradise itself through open gates. Here a totally other face of the entire Scripture showed itself to me. . . . I extolled my sweetest word with a love as great as the hatred with which I had before hated the word, 'righteousness of God.' Thus that place in Paul was for me truly the gate to paradise" (John Dillenberger, ed., *Martin Luther: Selections from His Writings* [Garden City, NY: Doubleday and Co., 1961], pp. 11-12). For a classic statement of this powerful doctrine of justification by faith alone, see James Buchanan, *The Doctrine of Justification* (Edinburgh: The Banner of Truth Trust, 1961, orig. 1867), or, in more recent years, R. C. Sproul, *Faith Alone: The Evangelical Doctrine of Justification* (Grand Rapids: Baker Book House, 1995).

are all our days and ways, did cast into my hand one day a book of Martin Luther's; it was his *Comment on Galatians. . . .* I found my condition in his experience so largely and profoundly handled, as if his book had been written out of my heart. . . . I do prefer this book of Martin Luther upon the Galatians, excepting the Holy Bible, before all the books that ever I have seen, as most fit for a wounded conscience."[29]

A Preacher Is Born

So in 1655 when the matter of his soul was settled, he was asked to exhort the church, and suddenly a great preacher was discovered. He would not be licensed as pastor of the Bedford church until seventeen years later. But his popularity as a powerful lay preacher exploded. The extent of his work grew. "When the country understood that . . . the tinker had turned preacher," John Brown tells us, "they came to hear the word by hundreds, and that from all parts."[30] Charles Doe, a comb maker in London, said (later in Bunyan's life), "Mr. Bunyan preached so New Testament-like he made me admire and weep for joy, and give him my affections."[31] In the days of toleration, a day's notice would get a crowd of 1,200 to hear him preach at 7 o'clock in the morning on a weekday.[32]

Once, while he was in prison, a whole congregation of sixty people was arrested and brought in at night. A witness tells us,

[29] *Grace Abounding*, pp. 52-53. Luther's *Commentary on Galatians* has been published in recent times with an introduction by D. Stuart Briscoe: *Martin Luther, Commentary on Galatians* (Old Tappan, NJ: Fleming H. Revell Co., 1998).
[30] John Brown, *John Bunyan*, p. 105.
[31] Ibid., p. 369.
[32] Ibid., p. 370.

"I . . . heard Mr. Bunyan both preach and pray with that mighty spirit of Faith and Plerophory [fullness] of Divine Assistance, that . . . made me stand and wonder."[33] The greatest Puritan theologian, and a contemporary of Bunyan, John Owen, when asked by King Charles why he, a great scholar, went to hear an uneducated tinker preach, said, "I would willingly exchange my learning for the tinker's power of touching men's hearts."[34]

The Incredible Elizabeth Bunyan

Ten years after they were married, when Bunyan was thirty, his wife died, leaving him with four children under ten, one of them blind. A year later, in 1659, he married Elizabeth, who was a remarkable woman. The year after their marriage, Bunyan was arrested and put in prison. She was pregnant with their firstborn and miscarried in the crisis. Then she cared for the four children as stepmother for twelve years alone and bore Bunyan two more children, Sarah and Joseph.

She deserves at least one story here—about her valor in going to the authorities in August 1661, a year after John's imprisonment. She had already been to London with one petition. Now she was met with one stiff question:

"Would he stop preaching?"

"My lord, he dares not leave off preaching as long as he can speak."

"What is the need of talking?"

"There is need for this, my lord, for I have four small

---

[33] Ibid., p. 160.
[34] Ibid., p. 366. This is a paraphrase of an indirect quote.

children that cannot help themselves, of which one is blind, and we have nothing to live upon but the charity of good people."

Matthew Hale, with pity, asks if she really has four children being so young.

"My lord, I am but mother-in-law [stepmother] to them, having not been married to him yet full two years. Indeed, I was with child when my husband was first apprehended; but being young and unaccustomed to such things, I being smayed at the news, fell into labor, and so continued for eight days, and then was delivered; but my child died."

Hale is moved, but other judges are hardened and speak against him. "He is a mere tinker!"

"Yes, and because he is a tinker and a poor man, therefore he is despised and cannot have justice."

One Mr. Chester is enraged and says Bunyan will preach and do as he wishes.

"He preacheth nothing but the word of God!" she says.

Mr. Twisden, in a rage: "He runneth up and down and doeth harm."

"No, my lord, it is not so; God hath owned him and done much good by him."

The angry man continues, "His doctrine is the doctrine of the devil."

She replies, "My lord, when the righteous Judge shall appear, it will be known that his doctrine is not the doctrine of the devil!"

Bunyan's biographer comments, "Elizabeth Bunyan was simply an English peasant woman: could she have spoken with more dignity had she been a crowned queen?"[35]

---

[35] Ibid., pp. 149-150.

Imprisoned from "My Poor Blind Child"

So for twelve years Bunyan chooses prison and a clear conscience over freedom and a conscience soiled by the agreement not to preach. He could have had his freedom when he wanted it. But he and Elizabeth were made of the same stuff. When asked to recant and not to preach he said,

> If nothing will do unless I make of my conscience a con- tinual butchery and slaughtershop, unless putting out my own eyes, I commit me to the blind to lead me, as I doubt not is desired by some, I have determined, the Almighty God being my help and shield, yet to suffer, if frail life might continue so long, even till the moss shall grow on mine eyebrows, rather than thus to violate my faith and principles.[36]

Nevertheless he was sometime tormented that he might not be making the right decision in regard to his family.

> The parting with my Wife and poor children hath often been to me in this place as the pulling of the Flesh from my bones; and that not only because I am somewhat too fond of these great Mercies, but also because I should have often brought to my mind the many hardships, mis- eries and wants that my poor Family was like to meet with should I be taken from them, especially my poor blind child, who lay nearer my heart than all I had besides; O the thoughts of the hardship I thought my Blind one might go under, would break my heart to pieces.[37]

---

[36] Ibid., p. 224.
[37] *Grace Abounding*, p. 123.

Persevering in Bedford, Not London

Yet he stayed. In 1672 he was released from prison because of the Declaration of Religious Indulgence. Immediately he was licensed as the pastor of the church in Bedford, which he had been serving all along, even from within prison, by writings and periodic visits. A barn was purchased and renovated as their first building, and this was where Bunyan ministered as pastor for the next sixteen years until his death. He never was wooed away from this little parish by the larger opportunities in London. The estimate is that, in 1676, there were perhaps 120 twenty nonconformist parishioners in Bedford, with others no doubt coming to hear him from the surrounding villages.

There was one more imprisonment in the winter and spring of 1675-76. John Brown thinks that this was the time when *The Pilgrim's Progress* was written. But even though Bunyan wasn't in prison again during his ministry, the tension of the days was extraordinary. Ten years after his last imprisonment in the mid-1680s, persecution was heavy again. "Richard Baxter [for example] though an old man now, was shut up in gaol, where he remained for two years more, and where he had innumerable companions in distress."[38]

Meetings were broken in upon, worshipers hurried to prison; "separatists changed the place of gathering from time to time, set their sentinels on the watch, left off singing hymns in their services, and for the sake of greater security worshiped

---

[38] Brown, *John Bunyan*, p. 336. Baxter was a Puritan pastor whose books are famous for their practical helpfulness even today. He was born in 1615 and died in 1691. His main parish was Kidderminster, where he preached and cared and catechized for twenty years. His most notable works include *The Reformed Pastor* and *The Saints' Everlasting Rest*.

again and again at the dead of night. Ministers were introduced to their pulpits through trap-doors in floor or ceiling, or through doorways extemporized in walls."[39] Bunyan expected to be taken away again. He deeded over all his possessions to his wife Elizabeth so that she would not be ruined by his fines or imprisonment.[40]

A Pilgrim Dies Away from Home

But God spared him. Until August 1688. In that month he traveled the fifty miles to London to preach and to help make peace between a man in his church and his alienated father. He was successful in both missions. But after a trip to an outlying district, he returned to London on horseback through excessive rains. He fell sick of a violent fever and on August 31, 1688, at age sixty, followed his famous fictional Pilgrim from the "City of Destruction" across the river into the "New Jerusalem."

His last sermon had been on August 19 in London at Whitechapel on John 1:13. His last words from the pulpit were, "Live like the children of God, that you may look your Father in the face with comfort another day."[41] His wife and children were probably unaware of the crisis until it was too late. So Bunyan, in all likelihood, died without the comfort of family— just as he had spent so much of his life without the comforts of home. "The inventory of Bunyan's property after his death added up to a total of 42 pounds and 19 shillings. This is more than the average tinker would leave, but it suggests that most of the profits from *The Pilgrim's Progress* had gone to printers of pirated editions."[42] He was born poor and never let himself become wealthy in this life. He is buried in London at Bunhill Fields.

So, in sum, we can include in Bunyan's sufferings the early, almost simultaneous, death of his mother and sister; the immediate remarriage of his father; the military draft in the midst of his teenage grief; the discovery that his first child was blind; the spiritual depression and darkness during the early years of his marriage; the death of his first wife, which left him with four small children; a twelve-year imprisonment, cutting him off from his family and church; the constant stress and uncertainty of imminent persecution, including one more imprisonment; and the final sickness and death far from those he loved most on earth. And this summary doesn't include any of the normal pressures and pains of ministry and marriage and parenting and controversy and criticism and sickness along the way.

Writing for the Afflicted Church

The question, then, that I bring to Bunyan's suffering is: What was its fruit? What did it bring about in his own life and, through him, in the lives of others? Knowing that I am leaving out many important things, I would answer that with five observations.

---

[42] Christopher Hill, *A Tinker and a Poor Man: John Bunyan and His Church, 1628-1688* (New York: Alfred A. Knopf, 1989), p. 367.

Bunyan's Suffering Confirmed Him in His Calling as a Writer, Especially for the Afflicted Church

Probably the greatest distortion of Bunyan's life in the portrait I have given so far in this chapter is that it passes over one of the major labors of his life, his writing. Books had awakened his own spiritual quest and guided him in it.[43] Books would be his main legacy to the church and the world.

Of course he is famous for *The Pilgrim's Progress*—"next to the Bible, perhaps the world's best-selling book . . . translated into over 200 languages."[44] It was immediately successful, with three editions in 1678, the first year it was published. It was despised at first by the intellectual elite, but as Lord Macaulay points out, "*The Pilgrim's Progress* is perhaps the only book about which, after the lapse of a hundred years, the educated minority has come over to the opinion of the common people."[45]

But most people don't know that Bunyan was a prolific writer before and after *The Pilgrim's Progress*. Christopher Hill's index of "Bunyan's Writings" lists fifty-eight books.[46] The variety in these books was remarkable: books dealing with controversies (like those concerning the Quakers and concerning justification and baptism), collections of poems, children's literature, and allegory (like *The Holy War* and *The Life and Death of Mr. Badman*). But the vast majority were practical doctrinal expositions of Scripture built from sermons for the sake of strengthening and

---

[43] See above, notes 17 and 28, and recall the role of *The Plain Man's Pathway to Heaven* and *The Practice of Piety* and Luther's *Commentary on Galatians*.

[44] Hill, *A Tinker and a Poor Man*, p. 375.

[45] Quoted in Barry Horner, *The Pilgrim's Progress by John Bunyan, Themes and Issues: An Evangelical Apologetic* (Lindenhurst, NY: Reformation Press Publishing, 1998), pp. 7-8.

[46] Hill, *A Tinker and a Poor Man*, pp. xv-xvii. *The Works of John Bunyan*, vol. 3, list 60, p. 763.

warning and helping Christian pilgrims make their way success-fully to heaven.

He was a writer from beginning to end. He had written four books before he went to prison at thirty-two, and in one year alone—1688, the year he died—five books were published. This is extraordinary for a man with no formal education. He knew nei-ther Greek nor Hebrew and had no theological degrees. This was such an offense in his own day that his pastor, John Burton, came to his defense, writing a foreword for his first book in 1656 (when Bunyan was twenty-eight): "This man is not chosen out of an earthly but out of the heavenly university, the Church of Christ. . . . He hath, through grace, taken these three heavenly degrees, to wit, union with Christ, the anointing of the Spirit, and experiences of the temptations of Satan, which do more fit a man for that mighty work of preaching the Gospel than all uni-versity learning and degrees that can be had."[47]

Bunyan's suffering left its mark on all his written work. George Whitefield said of *The Pilgrim's Progress*, "It smells of the prison. It was written when the author was confined in Bedford jail. And ministers never write or preach so well as when under the cross: the Spirit of Christ and of Glory then rests upon them."[48]

The smell of affliction was on most of what Bunyan wrote. In fact, I suspect that one of the reasons the Puritans are still being read today with so much profit is that their entire experi-ence, unlike ours, was one of persecution and suffering. To our chipper culture this may seem somber at times, but the day you

[47] *Some Gospel Truths Opened* in *The Works of John Bunyan*, vol. 2 (Edinburgh: The Banner of Truth Trust, 1991, orig. 1884), p. 141.
[48] Quoted in Horner, *The Pilgrim's Progress: An Evangelical Apologetic*, p. iii.

hear that you have cancer, or that your child is blind, or that a mob is coming, you turn away from the light books to the weighty ones that were written on the precipice of eternity where the fragrance of heaven and the stench of hell are both in the air.

Bunyan's writings were an extension of his pastoral ministry, mainly to his flock in Bedford, who lived in constant danger of harassment and prison. His suffering fit him well for the task. Which leads to the second effect of Bunyan's suffering I want to mention.

Bunyan's Suffering Deepened His Love for His Flock and Gave His Pastoral Labor the Fragrance of Eternity

His writings were filled with love to his people. For example, three years into his imprisonment he wrote a book for his own flock called *Christian Behavior*, which he ended like this:

> Thus have I, in a few words, written to you before I die, a word to provoke you to faith and holiness, because I desire that you may have the life that is laid up for all them that believe in the Lord Jesus, and love one another, when I am deceased. Though then I shall rest from my labors, and be in paradise, as through grace I comfortably believe, yet it is not there, but here, I must do you good. Wherefore, I, not knowing the shortness of my life, nor the hindrance that hereafter I may have of serving my God and you, I have taken this opportunity to present these few lines unto you for your edification.[49]

In his autobiography, written about halfway through his

---

[49] *Christian Behavior Being the Fruits of True Christianity,* in *The Works of John Bunyan,* vol. 2, p. 574.

imprisonment, he spoke of his church and the effect he hoped his possible martyrdom would have on them: "I did often say before the Lord, that if to be hanged up presently before their eyes would be means to awake in them and confirm them in the truth, I gladly should consent to it."[50] In fact, many of his flock joined him in jail, and he ministered to them there. He echoed the words of Paul when he described his longings for them: "In my preaching I have really been in pain, I have, as it were, travailed to bring forth Children to God."[51]

He gloried in the privilege of the gospel ministry. This too flowed from his suffering. If all is well and this world is all that matters, a pastor may become jealous of prosperous people who spend their time in leisure. But suffering abounds, and if prosperity is a cloak for the true condition of frisky, fun-loving, perishing Americans, then being a pastor may be the most important and glorious of all work. Bunyan thought it was: "My heart hath been so wrapped up in the glory of this excellent work, that I counted myself more blessed and honored of God by this, than if I had made me the emperor of the Christian world, or the lord of all the glory of the earth without it."[52]

He loved his people, he loved the work, and he stayed with it and with them to the end of his life. He served them and he served the world from a village parish with perhaps 120 members.

---

[50] Ibid., p. 110.
[51] Ibid.
[52] Ibid., p. 111.

Bunyan's Suffering Opened His Understanding to the
Truth That the Christian Life Is Hard and That
Following Jesus Means Having the Wind in Your Face

In 1682, six years before his death, he wrote a book called *The*
Greatness of the Soul based on Mark 8:36-37, "What does it profit
a man to gain the whole world, and forfeit his soul? For what will
a man give in exchange for his soul?" He says that his aim is to
"awaken you, rouse you off of your beds of ease, security, and pleasure, and fetch you down upon your knees before him, to beg of
him grace to be concerned about the salvation of your souls."[53]
And he does not mean the point of conversion, but the process of
perseverance. "The one who endures to the end, he will be saved"
(Mark 13:13). He hears Jesus warning us that life with him is hard:

> Following of me is not like following . . . some other mas-
> ters. The wind sits always on my face and the foaming rage
> of the sea of this world, and the proud and lofty waves
> thereof do continually beat upon the sides of the bark or
> ship that myself, my cause, and my followers are in; he
> therefore that will not run hazards, and that is afraid to
> venture a drowning, let him not set foot into this vessel.[54]

Two years later, commenting on John 15:2 ("Every branch
that bears fruit, He prunes"), he says, "It is the will of God, that
they that go to heaven should go thither hardly or with difficulty.
The righteous shall scarcely be saved. That is, they shall, but yet
with great difficulty, that it may be the sweeter."[55]

---

[53] *The Greatness of the Soul and Unspeakableness of the Loss Thereof*, in *The Works of John Bunyan*, vol. 1, p. 105.

[54] Ibid., p. 105.

[55] *Seasonable Counsel, Advice to Sufferers*, in *The Works of John Bunyan*, vol. 2, p. 725.

He had tasted this at the beginning of his Christian life and at every point along the way. In the beginning:

> My soul was perplexed with unbelief, blasphemy, hardness of heart, questions about the being of God, Christ, the truth of the word, and certainty of the world to come: I say, then I was greatly assaulted and tormented with atheism.[56]

> Of all the temptations that ever I met with in my life, to question the being of God and the truth of his gospel is the worst, and the worst to be borne.[57]

In *The Excellency of a Broken Heart* (the last book he took to the publisher) he says,

> Conversion is not the smooth, easy-going process some men seem to think. . . . It is wounding work, of course, this breaking of the hearts, but without wounding there is no saving. . . . Where there is grafting there is a cutting, the scion must be let in with a wound; to stick it on to the outside or to tie it on with a string would be of no use. Heart must be set to heart and back to back, or there will be no sap from root to branch, and this I say, must be done by a wound.[58]

Bunyan's suffering made him passionate about these things— and patient. You can hear his empathy with strugglers in these typ-

---

[56] *Grace Abounding*, p. 96.
[57] Ibid., p. 128.
[58] Quoted in Brown, *John Bunyan*, p. 373. See the fuller original in *The Acceptable Sacrifice: The Excellency of a Broken Heart*, in *The Works of John Bunyan*, vol. 1, p. 720.

ically earthy words in a book from 1678 called *Come and Welcome to Jesus Christ*:

> He that comes to Christ cannot, it is true, always get on as fast as he would. Poor coming soul, thou art like the man that would ride full gallop whose horse will hardly trot. Now the desire of his mind is not to be judged of by the slow pace of the dull jade he rides on, but by the hitching and kicking and spurring as he sits on his back. Thy flesh is like this dull jade, it will not gallop after Christ, it will be backward though thy soul and heaven lie at stake.[59]

It seems to me that Bunyan knew the balance of Philippians 2:12-13, "So then, my beloved . . . work out your salvation with fear and trembling; for it is God who is at work in you, both to will and to work for His good pleasure." First, he publishes a book called *Saved By Grace*[60] based on Ephesians 2:5, "By grace you have been saved." And then in the same year he follows it with a book called *The Strait Gate*,[61] based on Luke 13:24, "Strive to enter at the strait gate: for many, I say unto you, will seek to enter in, and shall not be able" (KJV).

Bunyan's sufferings had taught him the words of Jesus first-hand: "The way is hard that leads to life, and those who find it are few" (Matthew 7:14, RSV).[62]

---

[59] *Come and Welcome to Jesus Christ*, in *The Works of John Bunyan*, vol. 1, p. 252.

[60] *Saved by Grace*, in *The Works of John Bunyan*, vol. 1, pp. 335-361.

[61] *The Strait Gate*, in *The Works of John Bunyan*, vol. 1, pp. 362-390.

[62] For a serious meditation on this passage, see Benjamin Breckenridge Warfield, "Are They Few That Be Saved?" *Biblical and Theological Studies*, Samuel G. Craig, ed. (Philadelphia: The Presbyterian and Reformed Publishing Co., 1952), pp. 334-350.

Bunyan's Sufferings Strengthened His Assurance That God Is Sovereign over All the Afflictions of His People and Will Bring Them Safely Home

There have always been, as there are today, people who try to solve the problem of suffering by denying the sovereignty of God—that is, the all-ruling providence of God over Satan and over nature and over human hearts. But it is remarkable how many of those who stand by the doctrine of God's sovereignty over suffering have been those who suffered most and who found in the doctrine the most comfort and help.[63]

Bunyan was among that number. In 1684 he wrote an exposition for his suffering people based on 1 Peter 4:19, "Let them that suffer according to the will of God commit the keeping of their souls to him in well doing, as unto a faithful Creator" (KJV). The book was called *Seasonable Counsel, or Advice to Sufferers.* He takes the phrase "according to the will of God" and unfolds the sovereignty of God in it for the comfort of his people.

> It is not what enemies will, nor what they are resolved upon, but what God will, and what God appoints; that shall be done. . . . No enemy can bring suffering upon a man when the will of God is otherwise, so no man can save himself out of their hands when God will deliver him up for his glory . . . [just as Jesus showed Peter "by what death he would glorify God," John 21:19]. We shall or shall not suffer, even as it pleaseth him.[64]

---

[63] For examples, see Faith Cook, *Singing in the Fire* (Edinburgh: The Banner of Truth Trust, 1995), and "Suffering: The Sacrifice of Christian Hedonism," in John Piper, *Desiring God: Meditations of a Christian Hedonist* (Sisters, OR: Multnomah Publishers, 1996), pp. 212-238, and "The Supremacy of God in Missions Through Suffering," in *Let the Nations Be Glad: The Supremacy of God in Missions* (Grand Rapids, MI: Baker Book House, 1993), pp. 71-114.

[64] *Seasonable Counsel, or Advice to Sufferers,* p. 722. For a meditation on the theological problems involved with this biblical view, see John Piper, "The Pleasure of God in All That He Does," in *The Pleasures of God: Meditations on God's Delight in Being God* (Sisters, OR: Multnomah Publishers, 2000), pp. 47-78.

Thus God has appointed the persons who will suffer, the time of their suffering, the place of their suffering, and how they will suffer.

God Appoints Who Will Suffer

In the first case, "God has appointed *who* shall suffer. Suffering comes not by chance, or by the will of man, but by the will and appointment of God." Thus Bunyan cites 1 Thessalonians 3:3 (KJV): ". . . that no man should be moved by these afflictions: for yourselves know that we are appointed thereunto." We must not think that suffering is a strange thing for those who fear God (1 Peter 4:12), he reminds us and appeals to Revelation 6:11 where the martyrs under the altar in heaven are told "that they should rest for a little while longer, until the number of their fellow servants and their brethren who were to be killed ["mark that," Bunyan says] even as they had been, would be completed also." An appointed number of martyrs! From which Bunyan concludes, "Suffering for righteousness and for righteousness' sake, is by the will of God. God has appointed who shall suffer."[65]

"My Times Are in Thy Hands"

Secondly, "God has appointed . . . *when* they shall suffer for his truth in the world. Sufferings for such and such a man are timed, as to when he shall be tried for his faith." Hence when Paul was afraid in Corinth, the Lord strengthened him in a dream by saying, "Do not be afraid any longer, but go on speaking and do not

---

[65] *Seasonable Counsel*, p. 723.

be silent; for I am with you, and no man will attack you in order to harm you, for I have many people in this city" (Acts 18:9-10). "His time of suffering," Bunyan says, "was not yet come there." In the same way it was said of Jesus, "They sought to take him: but no man laid hands on him, because his hour was not yet come" (John 7:30, KJV). Bunyan concludes, "The times, then, and the seasons, even for the sufferings of the people of God, are not in the hands of their enemies, but in the hand of God; as David said, 'My times are in thy hand'" (Psalm 31:15).[66]

Suffering Saints Are Sprinkled on the Earth to Keep It from Stinking

Thirdly, "God has appointed *where* this, that or the other good man shall suffer. Moses and Elias [Elijah], when they appeared on the holy mount, told Jesus of the sufferings which he should accomplish at Jerusalem" (Luke 9:30-31). "The saints are sprinkled by the hand of God here and there, as salt is sprinkled upon meat to keep it from stinking. And as they are sprinkled, that they may season the earth; so accordingly, where they must suffer is also appointed for the better confirming of the truth. Christ said, it could not be that a prophet should 'perish out of Jerusalem' (Luke 13:33). But why . . . ? God has appointed that they should suffer there. So then, who, when, and where, is at the will of God, and they, accordingly, are ordered by that will."[67]

---

[66] Ibid., p. 723.
[67] Ibid.

"By What Death He Should Glorify God"

Fourth, "God has appointed . . . *what kind of sufferings* this or that saint shall undergo. . . . God said that he would show Paul beforehand how great things he should suffer for his sake (Acts 9:16). And it is said that Christ did signify to Peter beforehand 'by what death he should glorify God' (John 21:19)." As with the time and place and persons, so it is with the kind of sufferings we endure: They "are all writ down in God's book; and though the writing seem as unknown characters to us, yet God understands them very well. . . . It is appointed who of them should die of hunger, who with the sword, who should go into captivity, and who should be eaten up of beasts. Let it then be concluded, that hitherto it appears, that the sufferings of saints are ordered and disposed by the will of God." [68]

We could go even further with Bunyan as he shows "for what truth" his saints will suffer, and "by whose hand" and "how long." But let us ask, What is Bunyan's aim in this exposition of the sovereignty of God in suffering? He tells us plainly: "I have, in a few words, handled this . . . to show you that our sufferings are ordered and disposed by him, that you might always, when you come into trouble for this name, not stagger nor be at a loss, but be stayed, composed, and settled in your minds, and say, 'The will of the Lord be done.' Acts 21:14." [69]

---

[68] Ibid. Compare Jeremiah 15:2-3: "And it shall be that when they say to you, 'Where should we go?' then you are to tell them, 'Thus says the LORD: "Those destined for death, to death; and those destined for the sword, to the sword; and those destined for famine, to famine; and those destined for captivity, to captivity. I will appoint over them four kinds of doom," declares the LORD: "the sword to slay, the dogs to drag off, and the birds of the sky and the beasts of the earth to devour and destroy."'"

[69] Ibid., p. 724.

The Mercy That We Suffer Rather Than Torture

He warns against feelings of revenge.

> Learn to pity and bewail the condition of the enemy. . . .
> Never grudge them their present advantages. "Fret not thy
> self because of evil men. Neither be thou envious at the
> workers of iniquity." Proverbs 24:19. Fret not, though they
> spoil thy resting place. It is God that hath bidden them do
> it, to try thy faith and patience thereby. Wish them no ill
> with what they get of thine; it is their wages for their work,
> and it will appear to them ere long that they have earned it
> dearly. . . . Bless God that thy lot did fall on the other
> side. . . .[70] How kindly, therefore, doth God deal with us,
> when he chooses to afflict us but for a little, that with ever-
> lasting kindness he may have mercy upon us. Is. 54:7-8.[71]

"No Fruit, Because There Is no Winter There"

The key to suffering rightly is to see in all things the hand of a merciful and good and sovereign God and "to live upon God that is
invisible."[72] There is more of God to be had in times of suffering
than at any other time.

> There is that of God to be seen in such a day as cannot be
> seen in another. His power in holding up some, his wrath

---

[70] Ibid., p. 725.

[71] Ibid., p. 737. If one asks whether God is sovereign over the temptations of soul as well as
sufferings of body, Bunyan answers yes. Looking back on his own dark seasons of doubt and
despair he writes, "Now I saw that as God had his hand in all the providences and dispensations
that overtook his elect, so he had his hand in all the temptations that they had to sin against him,
not to animate them to wickedness, but to choose their temptations and troubles for them,
and also to leave them for a time to such things only as might not destroy, but humble them—
as might not put them beyond, but lay them in the way of the renewing of his mercy" *Grace
Abounding*, p. 61.

[72] *Grace Abounding*, p. 109.

in leaving of others; his making of shrubs to stand, and his suffering of cedars to fall; his infatuating of the counsel of men, and his making of the devil to outwit himself; his giving of his presence to his people, and his leaving of his foes in the dark; his discovering [disclosing] the uprightness of the hearts of his sanctified ones, and laying open the hypocrisy of others, is a working of spiritual wonders in the day of his wrath, and of the whirlwind and storm. . . . We are apt to overshoot, in the days that are calm, and to think ourselves far higher, and more strong than we find we be, when the trying day is upon us. . . . We could not live without such turnings of the hand of God upon us. We should be overgrown with flesh, if we had not our seasonable winters. It is said that in some countries trees will grow, but will bear no fruit, because there is no winter there.[73]

So Bunyan begs his people to humble themselves under the mighty hand of God and to trust that all will be for their good. "Let me beg of thee, that thou wilt not be offended either with God, or men, if the cross is laid heavy upon thee. Not with God, for he doth nothing without a cause, nor with men, for . . . they are the servants of God to thee for good. Take therefore what comes to thee from God by them, thankfully."[74]

"If It Is in Thy Heart to Fly, Fly"

If one should ask, may we ever, then, avail ourselves of opportunities to escape suffering, Bunyan answers,

---

[73] *Seasonable Counsel*, p. 694.
[74] Ibid.

Thou mayest do in this as it is in thy heart. If it is in thy heart to fly, fly; if it be in thy heart to stand, stand. Anything but a denial of the truth. He that flies, has warrant to do so; he that stands, has warrant to do so. Yea, the same man may both fly and stand, as the call and working of God with his heart may be. Moses fled, Exodus 2:15; Moses stood, Hebrews 11:27. David fled, 1 Samuel 19:12; David stood, 1 Samuel 24:8. Jeremiah fled, Jeremiah 37:11-12; Jeremiah stood, 38:17. Christ withdrew himself, Luke 19:10; Christ stood, John 18:1-8. Paul fled, 2 Cor. 11:33; Paul stood, Acts 20:22-23. . . .

There are few rules in this case. The man himself is best able to judge concerning his present strength, and what weight this or that argument has upon his heart to stand or fly. . . . Do not fly out of a slavish fear, but rather because flying is an ordinance of God, opening a door for the escape of some, which door is opened by God's providence, and the escape countenanced by God's Word. Matthew 10:23. . . . If, therefore, when thou hast fled, thou art taken, be not offended at God or man: not at God, for thou art his servant, thy life and thy all are his; not at man, for he is but God's rod, and is ordained, in this, to do thee good. Hast thou escaped? Laugh. Art thou taken? Laugh. I mean, be pleased which way soever things shall go, for that the scales are still in God's hand.[75]

This is what Bunyan means by "living upon God that is invisible." This is the faith that makes a person radically free and bold and undaunted in the cause of God and truth. Bunyan's life

---

[75] Ibid., p. 726.

did not arise out of sand. It grew like a great tree in the rock of granite truth about the sovereignty of God over all his suffering.

Bunyan's Suffering Deepened in Him a Confidence in the Bible as the Word of God and a Passion for Biblical Exposition as the Key to Perseverance

If "living upon God that is invisible" is the key to suffering rightly, what is the key to living upon God? Bunyan's answer is: Lay hold on Christ through the Word of God, the Bible. He doesn't mean this, of course, to the exclusion of prayer. In fact, he pleaded for his people to pray for him and confessed his utter dependence on God in prayer:

> Christians, pray for me to our God with much earnestness, fervency, and frequently in all your knockings at our Father's door, because I do very much stand in need thereof, for my work is great, my heart is vile, and the devil lieth at watch, the world would fain be saying, Aha, aha, thus would we have it! And of myself, keep myself I cannot, trust myself I dare not; if God do not help me I am sure it will not be long before my heart deceive, and the world have their advantage of me.[76]

Prison as an Inlet into the Word of God

But what we need most to hear from Bunyan is how his suffering drove him into the Word and opened the Word to him. Prison proved for Bunyan to be a hallowed place of communion with God because his suffering unlocked the Word and the deepest

---

[76] Brown, *John Bunyan*, p. 119.

fellowship with Christ he had ever known. Martin Luther said the same thing and even made it into a rule that suffering is essential to know the Word of God as we ought, basing it on Psalm 119:71, "It is good for me that I was afflicted, that I may learn Your statutes." Luther had his own scandalous way of saying it:

As soon as God's Word becomes known through you, the devil will afflict you, will make a real doctor [theologian or teacher] of you, and will teach you by his temptations to seek and to love God's Word. For I myself . . . owe my papists many thanks for so beating, pressing, and frightening me through the devil's raging that they have turned me into a fairly good theologian, driving me to a goal I should never have reached.[77]

Bunyan made the same discovery, as have so many others.[78]

I never had in all my life so great an inlet into the Word of God as now [in prison]. Those scriptures that I saw nothing in before were made in this place and state to shine upon me. Jesus Christ also was never more real and apparent than now. Here I have seen him and felt him indeed. . . . I have had sweet sights of the forgiveness of my sins in this place,

---

[77] Ewald M. Plass, comp., *What Luther Says: An Anthology*, vol. 3 (St. Louis: Concordia Publishing House, 1959), p. 1360. The reader may be interested in seeing more about how Luther came to this conviction and how it affected his life; see Piper, *The Legacy of Sovereign Joy: God's Triumphant Grace in the Lives of Augustine, Luther, and Calvin* (Wheaton, IL: Crossway Books, 2000).

[78] For example, John Paton, the Scottish missionary to the New Hebrides (Vanuatu) 100 years ago, described one of his most harrowing escapes from danger as he hid in a tree with cannibals raging around him: "Never, in all my sorrows, did my Lord draw nearer to me, and speak more soothingly in my soul, than when the moonlight flickered among these chestnut leaves, and the night air played on my throbbing brow, as I told all my heart to Jesus. Alone, yet not alone! If it be to glorify my God, I will not grudge to spend many nights alone in such a tree, to feel again my Savior's spiritual presence, to enjoy His consoling fellowship. If thus thrown back upon your own soul, alone, all alone, in the midnight, in the bush, in the very embrace of death itself, have you a Friend that will not fail you then?" *John G. Paton: Missionary to the New Hebrides, An Autobiography Edited by His Brother* (Edinburgh: The Banner of Truth Trust, 1965, orig. 1889, 1891), p. 200.

and of my being with Jesus in another world. . . . I have seen
that here that I am persuaded I shall never, while in this
world, be able to express. . . . I never knew what it was for
God to stand by me at all times and at every offer of Satan
to afflict me, as I have found Him since I came in hither.[79]

"In My Chest Pocket I Have a Key"

Bunyan especially cherished the promises of God as the key for opening the door of heaven. "I tell thee, friend, there are some promises
that the Lord hath helped me to lay hold of Jesus Christ through
and by, that I would not have out of the Bible for as much gold and
silver as can lie between York and London piled up to the stars."[80]

One of the greatest scenes in *The Pilgrim's Progress* is when
Christian recalls, in the dungeon of Doubting-Castle, that he has
a key to the door. Very significant is not only what the key is, but
where it is:

> "What a fool I have been, to lie like this in a stinking dun-
> geon, when I could have just as well walked free. In my
> chest pocket I have a key called Promise that will, I am thor-
> oughly persuaded, open any lock in Doubting-Castle."
> "Then," said Hopeful, "that is good news. My good
> brother, do immediately take it out of your chest pocket and
> try it." Then Christian took the key from his chest and
> began to try the lock of the dungeon door; and as he turned
> the key, the bolt unlocked and the door flew open with ease,
> so that Christian and Hopeful immediately came out.[81]

---

[79] *Grace Abounding*, p. 121.

[80] Bunyan, *Sighs from Hell*, in *The Works of John Bunyan*, vol. 3, p. 721.

[81] John Bunyan, *The Pilgrim's Progress*, Barry Horner, ed. (North Brunswick, NJ: n.p., 1997),
p. 172.

Three times Bunyan says that the key was in Christian's "*chest pocket*" or simply his "chest." I take this to mean that Christian had hidden it in his heart by memorization and that it was now accessible in prison (though he had no Bible available) for precisely this reason. This is how the Word sustained and strengthened Bunyan.

"Prick Him Anywhere . . . His Blood Is Bibline"

Everything he wrote was saturated with the Bible. He pored over his English Bible which was all he had most of the time. Which is why he can say of his writings, "I have not for these things fished in other men's waters; my Bible and Concordance are my only library in my writings."[82] The great London preacher Charles Spurgeon, who read *The Pilgrim's Progress* every year, put it like this:

> He had studied our Authorized Version . . . till his whole being was saturated with Scripture; and though his writings are charmingly full of poetry, yet he cannot give us his *Pilgrim's Progress*—that sweetest of all prose poems—without continually making us feel and say, "Why, this man is a living Bible!" Prick him anywhere; and you will find that his blood is Bibline, the very essence of the Bible flows from him. He cannot speak without quoting a text, for his soul is full of the Word of God.[83]

Bunyan reverenced the Word of God and trembled at the prospect of dishonoring it. "Let me die . . . with the Philistines

---

[82] Brown, *John Bunyan*, p. 364.
[83] Charles Spurgeon, *Autobiography*, vol. 2 (Edinburgh: The Banner of Truth Trust, 1973), p. 159.

(Judges 16:30) rather than deal corruptly with the blessed word of
God."[84] This, in the end, is why Bunyan is still with us today rather
than disappearing into the mist of history. He is with us and ministering to us because he reverenced the Word of God and was so
permeated by it that his blood is "Bibline"—the essence of the
Bible flows from him.

And this is what he has to show us. That "to live upon God
that is invisible" is to live upon the Word of God. To serve and suffer rooted in God is to serve and suffer saturated with the Word
of God. This is how we shall live, this is how we shall suffer.
And, if we are called to be leaders among the people of God, this
is how we shall help our people get safely to the Celestial City.
We will woo them with the Word. We will say to them what
Bunyan said to his people—and I say to you, dear reader:

> God hath strewed all the way from the gate of hell, where
> thou wast, to the gate of heaven, whither thou art going,
> with flowers out of his own garden. Behold how the
> promises, invitations, calls, and encouragements, like lilies,
> lie round about thee! Take heed that thou dost not tread
> them under thy foot.[85]

---

[84] Bunyan, *Grace Abounding*, p. 114.
[85] Quoted from *Come and Welcome to Jesus Christ* (1678), in Brown, *John Bunyan*, p. 300.

God moves in a mysterious way

His wonders to perform;

He plants his footsteps in the sea,

And rides upon the storm.

Ye fearful saints, fresh courage take,

The clouds ye so much dread

Are big with mercy, and shall break

In blessings on your head.

Judge not the lord by feeble sense,

But trust him for his grace;

Behind a frowning providence

He hides a smiling face.

His purposes will ripen fast,

Unfolding every hour;

The bud may have a bitter taste,

But sweet will be the flower.

WILLIAM COWPER
"GOD MOVES IN A MYSTERIOUS WAY"

2

"THE CLOUDS YE SO MUCH DREAD ARE BIG WITH MERCY"

Insanity and Spiritual Songs in the Life of William Cowper

A Love Affair with Poetry

There are at least three reasons why I am drawn to the life story of the eighteenth-century poet William Cowper (pronounced "Cooper"). One is that ever since I was seventeen—probably before—I have felt the power of poetry.

I went to my file recently and found an old copy of *Leaves of Grass*, the student literary magazine from Wade Hampton High School, Greenville, South Carolina. It was the 1964 edition—the year I graduated. I read the poems that I wrote for it more than thirty-five years ago. Then I took out *Kodon*, the literary magazine from my Wheaton College days, and remembered the poem "One of Many Lands," which I wrote in one of my bleak moments as a college freshman. Next, from the musty folder of memorabilia, came a copy of *The Opinion* (1969) from Fuller Seminary with its poem "For Perfect Eve" (to whom I have now been married thirty-two years). Then when I was teaching came the Bethel College *Coeval* from 1976 with the poem "Dusk." It struck me again what a longtime friend poetry has been. And still is. I write poems for my children's birthdays and for my wife on birthdays and anniversaries and Mother's Day. For almost twenty years I have written four Advent poems each year and read them from the pulpit to my much-loved flock at Bethlehem Baptist Church.

One of the reasons for this is that I live with an almost constant awareness of the breach between the low intensity of my own passion and the staggering realities of the universe around me—heaven, hell, creation, eternity, life, Jesus Christ, justification by faith, God. All of us (whether we know it or not) try to close this breach between the weakness of our emotions and the wonder of the world. Some of us do it with poetry.

William Cowper did it with poetry. I think I understand something of what he means, for example, when he writes a poem about seeing his mother's portrait after fifty-three years. She had died when he was six.

> And, while that face renews my filial grief,
> Fancy shall weave a charm for my relief.[1]

Fancy—the imaginative effort to put his emotion in a poem—will bring him some pleasant, painful satisfaction. There is a deep relief that comes when we find a way of seeing and savoring some precious reality, then saying it in a way that comes a little closer to closing the breach between what we've glimpsed with our mind and what we've grasped with out heart. It shouldn't be surprising that probably more than three hundred pages of the Bible were written as poetry, because one great aim of the Bible is to build a

---

[1] William Cowper, "On the Receipt of My Mother's Picture out of Norfolk," *The Poetical Works of William Cowper*, William Michael Rossetti, ed. (London: William Collins, Sons and Co., n.d.), p. 407.

bridge between the prosaic deadness of the human heart and the inexpressible reality of the living God.

The Man Who Wrote the Hymn Above Our Mantel

The second reason I am drawn to William Cowper is that I want to know the man behind the hymn "God Moves in a Mysterious Way," one of the last poems Cowper ever wrote. It appeared in the collection of "Olney Hymns" under the title "Conflict: Light Shining Out of Darkness." Over the years it has become very precious to me and many in our church. It has carried us through fire.

> *God moves in a mysterious way*
> *His wonders to perform;*
> *He plants his footsteps in the sea,*
> *And rides upon the storm.*
>
> *Deep in unfathomable mines*
> *Of never-failing skill,*
> *He treasures up his bright designs*
> *And works his sovereign will.*
>
> *Ye fearful saints, fresh courage take,*
> *The clouds ye so much dread*
> *Are big with mercy, and shall break*
> *In blessings on your head.*
>
> *Judge not the Lord by feeble sense,*
> *But trust him for his grace;*
> *Behind a frowning providence*
> *He hides a smiling face.*

His purposes will ripen fast,
Unfolding every hour;
The bud may have a bitter taste,
But sweet will be the flower.

Blind unbelief is sure to err,
And scan his work in vain:
God is his own interpreter,
And He will make it plain.[2]

For fourteen years an embroidered version of this hymn has hung in our living room. It was created and given to us by a young mother who was sustained by it through great sadness. It expresses the foundation of my theology and my life so well that I long to know the man who wrote it.

In the third place, I want to know why William Cowper struggled with depression and despair almost all his life. I want to try to come to terms with insanity and spiritual songs in the same heart of one whom I believe was a genuine Christian.

An Uneventful Life—On the Outside

Cowper was born in 1731 and died in 1800. That makes him a contemporary of John Wesley and George Whitefield, the leaders of the Evangelical Revival in England. He embraced Whitefield's Calvinistic theology rather than Wesley's Arminianism. But it was a warm, evangelical brand of Calvinism, shaped (in Cowper's case) largely by one of the healthiest men in the eighteenth century, the "old African blasphemer," John Newton. Cowper said he could

---

[2] Ibid., p. 292.

remember how, as a child, he would see the people at four o'clock in the morning coming to hear Whitefield preach in the open air. "Moorfields [was] as full of the lanterns of the worshipers before daylight as the Haymarket was full of flambeaux on opera nights."[3]

Cowper was twenty-seven years old when Jonathan Edwards died in America. He lived through the American and French revolutions. His poetry was known by Benjamin Franklin, who gave Cowper's first volume a good review.[4] But, though he was known internationally, he was not a man of affairs or travel. He was a recluse who spent virtually all his adult life in the rural English countryside near Olney and Weston.

From the standpoint of adventure or politics or public engagement, his life was utterly uneventful—the kind of life no child would ever choose to read about. But those of us who are older have come to see that the events of the soul are probably the most important events in life. And the battles in this man's soul were of epic proportions.

Consider, then, this seemingly uneventful life with a view to seeing the battles of the soul. He was born on November 15, 1731, at Great Berkhampstead, a town of about 1,500, near London. His father was rector of the village church and one of King George II's chaplains. So the family was well-to-do but not evangelical,[5] and William grew up without any saving relation to Christ.

---

[3] Gilbert Thomas, *William Cowper and the Eighteenth Century* (London: Ivor Nicholson and Watson, Ltd., 1935), p. 204.

[4] Ibid., p. 267.

[5] By this term I simply mean that the form of Christianity he imbibed at home did not highlight the "evangel," that is, the Gospel of Christ crucified and risen for sinners, which is recorded for us in the infallible Bible and preached in the power of the Holy Spirit, and believed in a very personal way that issues in a life of conscious devotion to Christ as the eternal Son of God, with disciplines of Bible reading and prayer and the pursuit of holiness and a concern for unbelievers to hear the Gospel and be saved from everlasting torment. Those would be the typical marks of an "evangelical" as I am using the term.

His mother died when he was six, and his father sent him to Pitman's, a boarding school in Bedfordshire. It was a tragic mistake, as we will see from his own testimony later in life. From the age of ten until he was seventeen he attended Westminster School and learned his French and Latin and Greek well enough to spend the last years of his life, fifty years later, translating the Greek of Homer and the French of Madam Guyon.

From 1749 he was apprenticed to a solicitor with a view to practicing law. At least this was his father's view. He never really applied himself and had no heart for the public life of a lawyer or a politician. For ten years he did not take his legal career seriously but lived a life of leisure with token involvement in his supposed career.

"Day and Night I Was Upon the Rack"

In 1752 he sank into his first paralyzing depression—the first of four major battles with mental breakdown so severe as to set him to staring out of windows for weeks at a time. Struggle with despair came to be the theme of his life. He was twenty-one years old and not yet a believer. He wrote about the attack of 1752 like this:

> [I was struck] with such a dejection of spirits, as none but they who have felt the same, can have the least conception of. Day and night I was upon the rack, lying down in horror, and rising up in despair. I presently lost all relish for those studies, to which before I had been closely attached; the classics had no longer any charms for me; I had need of

something more salutary than amusement, but I had no one to direct me where to find it.[6]

He came through this depression with the help of the poems of George Herbert (who had lived 150 years earlier, 1593-1633). "He found the hymns 'uncouth' and 'Gothic,' yet they spoke to his soul."[7] We are not told which of Herbert's poems broke through to Cowper with light, but there is one that has done so for me, and I like to think it did the same for Cowper. It is called "The Pulley." What makes it so relevant for Cowper's condition is Herbert's insight into how God, at times, withholds rest from our soul, not to make us miserable, but that restlessness may toss us to his breast.

> *Having a glass of blessings standing by,*
> *"Let us," said he, "pour on him all we can;*
> *Let the world's riches, which dispersed lie,*
> *Contract into a span."*
>
> *So strength first made a way;*
> *Then beauty flow'd, then wisdom, honour, pleasure;*
> *When almost all was out, God made a stay,*
> *Perceiving that alone of all his treasure,*
> *Rest in the bottom lay.*
>
> *"For if I should," said he,*
> *"Bestow this jewel also on my creature,*
> *He would adore my gifts instead of me,*
> *And rest in Nature, not the God of Nature:*
> *So both should losers be.*

---

[6] Thomas, *William Cowper and the Eighteenth Century*, p. 94.
[7] George Melvyn Ella, *William Cowper: Poet of Paradise* (Durham, England: Evangelical Press, 1993), p. 60.

"Yet let him keep the rest,
But keep them with repining restlessness;
Let him be rich and weary, that at least,
If goodness lead him not, yet weariness
May toss him to my breast."[8]

A Change of Scenery Does Not Heal

Throughout Cowper's life, God would have his strange means of tossing this stormy soul again and again back to his breast. In 1752, there was enough grace in the truth and beauty in the poems of George Herbert that Cowper felt hope and got the strength to take several months away from London by the sea in Southampton. What happened there was both merciful and sad. He wrote in his *Memoir*:

> The morning was calm and clear; the sun shone bright upon the sea; and the country on the borders of it was the most beautiful I had ever seen. . . . Here it was, that on a sudden, as if another sun had been kindled that instant in the heavens, on purpose to dispel sorrow and vexation of spirit, I felt the weight of all my weariness taken off; my heart became light and joyful in a moment; I could have wept with transport had I been alone.[9]

That was the mercy. The sadness of it was that even though he said, at the time, that "nothing less than the Almighty fiat could have filled me with such inexpressible delight,"[10] nevertheless he confessed later that instead of giving God the credit for this mercy,

[8] George Herbert, "The Pulley," in *Eerdmans Book of Christian Poetry*, comp. Pat Alexander (Grand Rapids, MI: William B. Eerdmans Publishing Co., 1981), p. 28.
[9] Thomas, *William Cowper and the Eighteenth Century*, p. 94.
[10] Ella, *William Cowper: Poet of Paradise*, p. 62.

he formed the habit merely of battling his depression, if at all, by seeking changes of scenery. It was the merciful hand of God in nature. But he did not see him or give him glory. Not yet.

Theodora Lost

Between 1749 and 1756, Cowper was falling in love with his cousin Theodora, whose home he visited regularly on the weekends. They were engaged, but for some mysterious reason her father, Ashley Cowper, forbade the marriage. His apparent reason was the inappropriateness of consanguinity—a man marrying his own cousin. But it seems strange that the relation was allowed to develop for seven years, as well as to move into an engagement, if it was to be shattered at the last minute. It is probably true that her father knew things about William that convinced him he would not have been a good husband for his daughter.

But it didn't turn out the way her father hoped. Though the pair never saw each other again after 1756, Theodora outlived William, but never married. She followed his poetic career from a distance and sent him money anonymously when he was in need, even a regular stipend at one point. We know of nineteen poems that he wrote to her as "Delia." One of them, written some years after their parting, shows the abiding pain:

> But now, sole partner in my Delia's heart,
> Yet doomed far off in exile to complain,
> Eternal absence cannot ease my smart,
> And hope subsists but to prolong my pain.[11]

---

[11] Cowper, *The Poetical Works*, p. 253.

What we will find is that William Cowper's life seems to be one long accumulation of pain.

As "at the Place of Execution"

In 1759, when he was twenty-eight years old, he was appointed, through the influence of his father, to be Commissioner of Bankrupts in London. Four years later he was about to be made Clerk of Journals in Parliament. What would have been a great career advancement to most men struck fear into William Cowper—so much so that he had a total mental breakdown, tried three different ways to commit suicide, and was put into an asylum.

His father had arranged for the position. But his enemies in Parliament decided to require a public interrogation for his son as a prerequisite. Cowper wrote about the dreadful attack of 1863:

> All the horrors of my fears and perplexities now returned.
> A thunderbolt would have been as welcome to me as this
> [interrogation]. . . . Those whose spirits are formed like
> mine, to whom a public exhibition of themselves, on any
> occasion, is mortal poison, may have some idea of the
> horror of my situation; others can have none.[12]

For more than half a year, his feelings were those "of a man when he arrives at the place of execution."[13]

At that point something dreadful returned to his memory that causes us to wonder about what kind of father William Cowper

---

[12] Thomas, *William Cowper and the Eighteenth Century*, p. 114.
[13] Ibid.

had. The thirty-two-year-old clerk suddenly recalled a "treatise on self-murder" that he read when he was eleven years old.

> I well recollect when I was about eleven years of age, my father desired me to read a vindication of self-murder, and give him my sentiments upon the question: I did so, and argued against it. My father heard my reasons, and was silent, neither approving nor disapproving; from whence I inferred that he sided with the author against me.[14]

In the week before his examination (October 1763) he bought laudanum to use as a poison. He pondered escaping to France to enter a monastery. He had illusions of seeing himself slandered in the newspaper anonymously. He was losing his hold on reality almost entirely. The day before the Parliamentary examination he set out to drown himself and took a cab to Tower Wharf. But at Custom House Quay he found the water too low and "a porter seated upon some goods" as if "a message to prevent" him.[15]

When he got home that evening he tried to take the laudanum but found his fingers "closely contracted" and "entirely useless." The next morning he tried three times to hang himself with a garter. The third time he became unconscious, but the garter broke. The laundress found him in bed and called his uncle who canceled the examination immediately. And that was the end of Cowper's brush with public life—but not the end of his brush with death.

Now came the horrible conviction of sin, as Cowper contemplated that he was as guilty as if he had succeeded with self-murder because he attempted and simply failed:

---

[14] Ibid., p. 118.
[15] Ibid.

Conviction of sin took place, especially of that just committed; the meanness of it, as well as its atrocity, were exhibited to me in colors so inconceivably strong that I despised myself, with a contempt not to be imagined or expressed. . . . This sense of it secured me from the repetition of a crime which I could not now reflect on without abhorrence. Before I rose from bed, it was suggested to me that there was nothing wanted but murder, to fill up the measures of my iniquities; and that, though I had failed in my design, yet I had all the guilt of that crime to answer for. A sense of God's wrath, and a deep despair of escaping it, instantly succeeded. The fear of death became much more prevalent in me than ever the desire of it had been.[16]

Now everything he read condemned him. Sleep would not come, and when it did, it brought him terrifying dreams. When he awoke he "reeled and staggered like a drunken man."[17]

Bless You, Insane Asylum, for My Life

So in December 1763 he was committed to St. Albans Insane Asylum, where the fifty-eight-year-old Dr. Nathaniel Cotton tended the patients. Cotton was somewhat of a poet, but most of all, by God's wonderful design, an evangelical believer and a lover of God and the Gospel. He loved Cowper and held out hope to him repeatedly in spite of his insistence that he was damned and beyond hope. Six months into his stay, Cowper found a Bible lying (not by accident) on a bench.

---

[16] Ibid., p. 119.
[17] Ibid., p. 120.

Having found a Bible on the bench in the garden, I opened upon the 11th of St. John, where Lazarus is raised from the dead; and saw so much benevolence, mercy, goodness, and sympathy with miserable men, in our Saviour's conduct, that I almost shed tears upon the revelation; little thinking that it was an exact type of the mercy which Jesus was on the point of extending towards myself. I sighed, and said, "Oh, that I had not rejected so good a Redeemer, that I had not forfeited all his favours." Thus was my heart softened, though not yet enlightened.[18]

Increasingly, he felt he was not utterly forsaken. Again he felt led to turn to the Bible. The first verse he saw was Romans 3:25: "Whom God hath set forth to be a propitiation through faith in his blood, to declare his righteousness for the remission of sins that are past, through the forbearance of God" (KJV).

Immediately I received the strength to believe it, and the full beams of the Sun of Righteousness shone upon me. I saw the sufficiency of the atonement He had made, my pardon sealed in His blood, and all the fullness and completeness of His justification. In a moment I believed, and received the gospel. . . . Whatever my friend Madan[19] had said to me, long before, revived in all its clearness, with demonstration of the spirit and with power. Unless the Almighty arm had been under me, I think I should have died with gratitude and joy. My eyes filled with tears, and

---

[18] Ibid., pp. 131-132.

[19] His cousin, Martin Madan, was an evangelical pastor. He had tried to encourage Cowper before his entering St. Albans, speaking to him earnestly of original sin, which gave him some hope, putting him more on a level with the rest of mankind rather than singled out for disfavor. He spoke to him of the all-atoning blood of Christ and the necessity of a lively faith in Christ. Cowper had only cried out that he wished God would work in his life. Ella, *William Cowper: Poet of Paradise*, p. 87.

my voice choked with transport; I could only look up to heaven in silent fear, overwhelmed with love and wonder.[20]

He had come to love St. Albans and Dr. Cotton so much that he stayed on another twelve months after his conversion. One might wish the story were one of emotional triumph after his conversion. But it did not turn out that way. Far from it.

The Sweet Mercy of a Slave-trading Seaman

In June 1765, Cowper left St. Albans and moved in with the Unwin family in Huntingdon. Mary Unwin was only eight years older than Cowper, but she was to become to him like a mother for almost thirty years. In 1767 Mr. Morley Unwin, Mary's husband, died in a tragic fall from his horse. Cowper lived in Mary Unwin's house for the rest of her life. This was significant not only because she was so caring of Cowper, but also because it set the stage for the most important relationship in Cowper's life—his friendship with John Newton.

John Newton was the curate at the church in Olney, not far from the Unwins' home. He had lost his mother when he was six, just like Cowper. But after being sent to school for a few years, he traveled with his father on the high seas, eventually becoming a slave-trading seaman himself. He was powerfully converted, and God called him to the ministry. He had been at Olney since 1764 and would be there till 1780.

We know him mainly as the author of "Amazing Grace." But

---

[20] Thomas, *William Cowper and the Eighteenth Century*, p. 132.

we should also know him as one of the healthiest, happiest pastors in the eighteenth century. Some said that other pastors were respected by their people, but Newton was loved. To illustrate the kind of spirit he had, here is a quote that gets at the heart of how he approached the ministry:

> Two heaps of human happiness and misery; now if I can take but the smallest bit from one heap and add to the other, I carry a point. If, as I go home, a child has dropped a halfpenny, and if, by giving it another, I can wipe away its tears, I feel I have done something. I should be glad to do greater things, but I will not neglect this. When I hear a knock on my study door, I hear a message from God; it may be a lesson of instruction, perhaps a lesson of penitence; but, since it is *his* message, it must be interesting.[21]

John Newton was told that a family near his parish had lost their father and husband—the Unwins. He made the trip to them and was such a help to them that they decided to move to Olney and sit under his ministry. So in September 1767 they moved from Huntingdon to Olney and lived in a place called Orchard Side for almost twenty years. For thirteen of those years, Newton was Cowper's pastor and counselor and friend. Cowper said, "A sincerer or more affectionate friend no man ever had."[22]

---

[21] Ibid., p. 202.
[22] Ibid., p. 192.

The Olney Hymns as Therapy

Newton saw Cowper's bent to melancholy and reclusiveness and drew him into the ministry of visitation as much as he could. They would take long walks together between homes and talk of God and his purposes for the church. Then, in 1769, Newton got the idea of collaborating with Cowper on a book of hymns to be sung by their church. He thought it would be good for Cowper's poetic bent to be engaged.

In the end, Newton wrote about two hundred of the hymns, and Cowper wrote sixty-eight. The hymnal was published in 1779. Besides "Amazing Grace," Newton wrote "How Sweet the Name of Jesus Sounds" and "Glorious Things of Thee Are Spoken" and "Come, My Soul, Thy Suit Prepare." Cowper wrote "God Moves in a Mysterious Way" and "There Is a Fountain Filled with Blood" and "O for a Closer Walk with God."

Nature "Became a Universal Blank"

But before Cowper could complete his share, he had what he called "the fatal dream." January had come again. His breakdowns had always been at their worst in January. And it was now ten years since "the dreadful '63." They came virtually every ten years in their most intense form. He does not say precisely what the dream was, but only that a "word" was spoken that reduced him to spiritual despair, something to the effect of "It is all over with you, you are lost."[23]

Twelve years later he still shuddered at the dream. He wrote

---

[23] Ibid., p. 225.

to Newton in 1785, "I had a dream twelve years ago before the recollection of which all consolation vanishes, and, it seems to me, must always vanish." Not long before his death he told Lady Hesketh, "In one day, in one *minute* I should rather have said, [Nature] became a universal blank to me; and though from a different cause, yet with an effect as difficult to remove, as blindness itself."[24]

Again there were repeated attempts at suicide, and each time God providentially prevented him. Newton stood by him all the way through this, even sacrificing at least one vacation so as not to leave Cowper alone.

In 1780, Newton left Olney for a new pastorate in Lombard Street, London, where he served for the next twenty-seven years. It is a great tribute to him that he did not abandon his friendship with Cowper, though this would, no doubt, have been emotionally easy to do. Instead there was an earnest exchange of letters for twenty years. Cowper poured out his soul to Newton as to no one else.

"Truths . . . Couched in Prose, They Would Not Hear"

Perhaps it was good for Newton to go away, because when he left, Cowper poured himself into his major poetic projects (between 1780 and 1786). Most of us today have never heard of any of these poems. His most famous and lengthy was called *The Task*, a 100-page poem in blank verse. Even though he saw himself, in his blackest moods, as reprobate and hopeless, he never stopped

---

[24] Ibid., p. 226.

believing in the truth of the Evangelical Awakening. All his poems are meant to teach as well as to entertain.

He wrote about himself:

> . . . I, who scribble rhyme
> To catch the triflers of the time,
> And tell them truths divine and clear
> Which, couched in prose, they would not hear.[25]

His first volume of poems was published in 1782 when he was fifty-one. Three years later came *The Task*, which established his fame. The great usefulness of these poems is that they "helped to spread [the Awakening's] ideas among the educated of all classes. . . . Because of his formal alliance with the [Evangelical] movement and the practical effects of his work, [Cowper] remains its [poet] laureate."[26]

Perhaps the productivity staved off the threatened breakdown of 1783, the next ten-year interval. But the reprieve did not last. In 1786 Cowper entered his fourth deep depression and again tried unsuccessfully to commit suicide. He and Mary moved from Olney to Weston that year, and the long decline of both of them began. He cared for her as for a dying mother from 1790 to 1796—filling what moments he could with work on his translations of Homer and other Greek (and French) works. He wrote his last original poem in 1799, called "The Castaway," and then died, apparently in utter despair, in 1800.

---

[25] Ibid., p. 265.
[26] Ibid., p. 183.

Reflections on His Depression

William Cowper's melancholy is disturbing. We need to come to terms with it in the framework of God's sovereign power and grace to save and sanctify his people. What are we to make of this man's lifelong battle with depression, and indeed his apparent surrender to despair and hopelessness in his own life?

One thing to notice is that there is some inconsistency in the way he reports his misery and hopelessness. For example, in a letter to John Newton on January 13, 1784, he wrote,

> Loaded as my life is with despair, I have no such comfort as would result from a supposed probability of better things to come, were it once ended. . . . You will tell me that this cold gloom will be succeeded by a cheerful spring, and endeavour to encourage me to hope for a spiritual change resembling it—but it will be lost labour. Nature revives again; but a soul once slain lives no more. . . . My friends, I know, expect that I shall see yet again. They think it necessary to the existence of divine truth, that he who once had possession of it should never finally lose it. I admit the solidity of this reasoning in every case but my own. And why not in my own? . . . I forestall the answer: God's ways are mysterious, and He giveth no account of His matters—an answer that would serve my purpose as well as theirs that use it. There is a mystery in my destruction, and in time it shall be explained.[27]

Notice that he affirms the truth of the doctrine of the perseverance of God's saints and does not even quarrel with the reality of his own conversion at St. Albans. What he disputes is that

---

[27] Ibid., pp. 281-282.

the general truth applies to him. He is the lone exception in the universe. He is reprobate, though once he was elect. Ask not why. God gives no account. This is the bleakest way possible of talking. It cuts off all reasoning and exhortation.

All Is Not Night

But notice something else. In that same year he was writing *The Task*. In it he recounts what Christ meant to him in a way that makes it very hard to believe there are no times now when this is still real for him:

> I was a stricken deer, that left the herd
> Long since; with many an arrow deep infixt
> My panting side was charg'd, when I withdrew
> To seek a tranquil death in distant shades.
> There was I found by one who had himself
> Been hurt by th' archers. In his side he bore,
> And in his hands and feet, the cruel scars.
> With gentle force soliciting the darts,
> He drew them forth, and heal'd, and bade me live.
> Since then, with few associates, in remote
> And silent woods I wander, far from those
> My former partners of the peopled scene;
> With few associates, and not wishing more.[28]

What would he mean in 1784, twelve years after the "fatal dream," that Jesus had drawn the arrows out and healed him

---

[28] Ibid., p. 302.

and bade him live? Were there not moments when he truly felt this and affirmed it against the constitutional gloom of his own mind?

Even in the 1790s there were expressions of hope. From time to time he gave evidence, for example, that he was permitted by God "once more to approach Him in prayer." His earliest biographer and friend said that in the days of that last decade God had once more opened a passage for him, but that "spiritual hounds" haunted him at night.[29]

And there was horrible blackness for him much of the time. He wrote to John Newton (friend to the end!) in 1792 that he always seemed to be "scrambling in the dark, among rocks and precipices, without a guide. Thus I have spent twenty years, but thus I shall not spend twenty years more. Long ere that period arrives, the grand question concerning my everlasting weal or woe will be decided."[30] This is bleak, but it is not the settled reprobation we read about in 1786.

A Castaway?

Three years later on March 20, 1799, he wrote his last original poem, with the seemingly hopeless title "The Castaway." It tells the story of a sailor washed overboard in a storm. His comrades desperately try to throw him something to hold on to. But the ship cannot be stopped in the wind and leaves the castaway behind, treading water in the darkness. He survives for an hour calling out in vain. Then "by toil subdued, he drank / The stifling wave, and then he sank."

---

[29] Ibid., pp. 368, 374.
[30] Ibid., p. 376.

This is clearly meant by Cowper to be a parable of his own forsaken and doomed condition. The last two verses make the application to himself:

> *I therefore purpose not, or dream*
> *Descanting on his fate,*
> *To give the melancholy theme*
> *A more enduring date:*
> *But misery still delights to trace*
> *Its semblance in another's case.*
>
> *No voice divine the storm allayed,*
> *No light propitious shone,*
> *When, snatched from all effectual aid,*
> *We perished, each alone:*
> *But I beneath a rougher sea,*
> *And whelmed in deeper gulfs than he.*[31]

There is something paradoxical about this statement of despair. The fact that he wrote it at all shows that his spirit was not wholly paralyzed with meaninglessness and emptiness. He is still strangely alert and responsive to the world. A man cannot write a beautiful poem who has lost all his joy in beauty. What kind of "misery" is it that "still delights"?

> *But misery still delights to trace*
> *Its semblance in another's case.*

This remnant of delight and this alertness to spiritual reality and poetic form seem to point to something less than absolute des-

---

[31] Cowper, *The Poetical Works*, p. 426.

olation. Moreover, there is another pointer. The title of the poem is significant. At least once before he had used the word "castaway" in a poem—Olney Hymn 36, "Welcome Cross." The poem magnifies the mercy and goodness of God in the trials he designs for us here. It ends,

> *Did I meet no trials here,*
> *No chastisement by the way,*
> *Might I not with reason fear*
> *I should prove a castaway?*
> *Bastards may escape the rod,*
> *Sunk in earthly vain delight;*
> *But the true-born child of God*
> *Must not—would not, if he might.*

Here the word "castaway" is taken from 1 Corinthians 9:27, "But I keep under my body, and bring it into subjection: lest that by any means, when I have preached to others, I myself should be a castaway" (KJV). Here the inescapable trials and chastisements are made an argument not that he is a castaway but that he is not. He is, rather, a true-born child of God. We do well, therefore, to put a question mark of doubt over the darkness with which Cowper cloaks his final days.

The last days of his life seemed to bring no relief in his sense of forsakenness. No happy ending. In March of 1800 he said to visiting Dr. Lubbock, "I feel unutterable despair." On April 24 Miss Perowne offered some refreshment to him, to which he replied, "What can it signify?" He never spoke again and died the next afternoon.[32]

---

[32] Thomas, *William Cowper and the Eighteenth Century*, p. 384.

The Roots of Gloom

What were the roots of such overwhelming and intractable gloom? No doubt there are secrets that God only knows. But we can see some reasons why he may have struggled the way he did.

Consider the home into which he was born. His father, John, married his mother, Ann, in 1728. Between the wedding in 1728 and his birth in 1731, three children had already been born and lost. He lives. But between 1731 and 1736, when his brother John was born, two more children enter the family and then die. Then his mother dies a few days after John's birth. William is six years old. The marriage is one sustained heartache.

The pain and emotional trauma of the death of his mother can probably not be calculated. It's true that the happy, healthy, well-adjusted John Newton also lost his mother at the age of six, the very year Cowper was born. But there is a difference, as we will see in a moment.

"Dupe of To-morrow Even from a Child"

In 1790, at the age of fifty-nine, Cowper received in the mail a portrait of his mother that swept him away with the emotion of years. He had not laid eyes on her face for fifty-three years. He wrote a poem to capture and release the pain and the pleasure of that "meeting." We catch a glimpse of what it was for him at age six to have lost his mother. And perhaps why he took so to Mrs. Mary Unwin.

Oh that those lips had language! Life has passed
With me but roughly since I heard thee last.

My mother! when I learned that thou wast dead,
Say, wast thou conscious of the tears I shed?
Hovered thy spirit o'er thy sorrowing son,
Wretch even then, life's journey just begun?

I heard the bell tolled on thy burial day,
I saw the hearse that bore thee slow away,
And turning from my nursery window, drew
A long, long sigh, and wept a last adieu!

Thy maidens, grieved themselves at my concern,
Oft gave me promise of thy quick return.
What ardently I wished, I long believed,
And disappointed still, was still deceived;
By expectation every day beguiled,
Dupe of to-morrow even from a child.

But the record fair,
That memory keeps of all thy kindness there,
Still outlives many a storm, that has effaced
A thousand other themes less deeply traced.
Thy nightly visits to my chamber made
That thou mightst know me safe and warmly laid;
Thy morning bounties ere I left my home,
Thy biscuit, or confectionery plum;
The fragrant waters on my cheeks bestowed
By thy own hand, till fresh they shone and glowed:
All this, and more endearing still than all,
Thy constant flow of love, that knew no fall,
Ne'er roughened by those cataracts and breaks,
That humour interposed too often makes:

All this still legible in memory's page,
And still to be so to my latest age.[33]

One begins to ponder the strange relations Cowper had all his life with older women, wanting them in his life, and yet causing them great confusion with the love poems he would write when he had no romantic intentions. Lady Austen in particular was bewildered by the way Cowper wrote to her.[34] This kind of behavior may have had its roots not only in the loss of his mother, but in the virtual loss of his father and his horrible experience in boarding school between the ages of six and eight.

Should Fathers Say, "Go Thither Where the Quicksands Lay"?

He hated boarding school and longed for his father:

> But my chief affliction consisted in my being singled out from all the other boys, by a lad about fifteen years of age as a proper object upon which he might let loose the cruelty of his temper. I choose to forbear a particular recital of the many acts of barbarity, with which he made it his business continually to persecute me: it will be sufficient to say, that he had, by his savage treatment of me, impressed such a dread of his figure upon my mind, that I well remember being afraid to lift up my

---

[33] Cowper, *The Poetical Works*, pp. 406-409.

[34] One writer says that his attitudes toward women were "simple as an infant." I would call them insensitive and unhealthy. In the summer of 1781, Cowper was introduced to the widow of Sir Robert Austen. She soon became "sister Ann" and more. She probably fell in love with him and cannot be blamed for thinking that he reciprocated. After two months, he wrote her not to think it romance. Later she came to Olney, and even stayed in Orchard Side because of an illness. She and Cowper had much time together in those days, and he wrote at least one very gallant poem for her that would have given any woman the thought of romance. But he had to write her again in the spring of 1784 to "renounce her society." There was no reconciliation this time. Cowper never met her again after 1784. She had inspired *John Gilpin* and *The Task*, but now she was gone. See Thomas, *William Cowper and the Eighteenth Century*, pp. 289-290.

eyes upon him, higher than his knees; and that I knew him by his shoe-buckles, better than any other part of his dress. May the Lord pardon him, and may we meet in glory![35]

One would never have said it in the eighteenth century. But knowing what we know today about its effects and what we know about boys at that age, it is hard not to raise the specter of sexual abuse. What horrors a little six-year-old boy may have experienced, combined with the loss of his mother and the virtual loss of his father!

Perhaps the most poignant lines Cowper ever wrote are hidden away in a poem called "Tirocinium" (Latin for the state of a new recruit—inexperienced, raw) in which he pleads for a private education rather than one at boarding school. What comes through here is a loud cry for his father to have been there for him, and a powerful plea to fathers even in the twenty-first century to be there for our children:

> *Would you your son should be a sot or dunce,*
> *Lascivious, headstrong, or all these at once,*
> *That in good time, the stripling's finished taste*
> *For loose expense and fashionable waste*
> *Should prove your ruin, and his own at last,*
> *Train him in public with a mob of boys,*
> *Childish in mischief only and in noise,*
> *Else of a mannish growth, and five in ten*
> *In infidelity and lewdness, men.*
> *There shall he learn, ere sixteen winters old,*
> *That authors are most useful, pawned or sold,*

---

[35] Ibid., pp. 69-70.

That pedantry is all that schools impart,
But taverns teach the knowledge of the heart.[36]

And seems it nothing in a father's eye
That unimproved those many moments fly?
And is he well content, his son should find
No nourishment to feed his growing mind
But conjugated verbs, and nouns declined?
For such is all the mental food purveyed
By public hackneys in the schooling trade.
Who feed a pupil's intellect with store
Of syntax truly, but with little more,
Dismiss their cares when they dismiss their flock,
Machines themselves, and governed by a clock.
Perhaps a father blest with any brains
Would deem it no abuse or waste of pains,
To improve this diet at no great expense,
With savoury truth and wholesome common sense,
To lead his son for prospects of delight
To some not steep though philosophic height,
Thence to exhibit to his wondering eyes
Yon circling worlds, their distance, and their size.[37]

To show him in an insect or a flower
Such microscopic proofs of skill and power,
As hid from ages past, God now displays
To combat atheists with in modern days.[38]

[O Father] Nature pulling at thine heart,
Condemns the unfatherly, the imprudent part.
Thou wouldst not, deaf to nature's tenderest plea,

---

[36] Cowper, *The Poetical Works*, p. 223.
[37] Ibid., p. 231.
[38] Ibid., p. 232.

Turn him adrift upon a rolling sea,
Nor say, go thither, conscious that there lay
A brood of asps, or quicksands in his way;
Then only governed by the self-same rule
Of natural pity, send him not to school.
No—Guard him better: Is he not thine own,
Thyself in miniature, thy flesh, thy bone?
And hopest thou not ('tis every father's hope)
That since thy strength must with thy years elope,
And thou wilt need some comfort to assuage
Health's last farewell, as staff of thine old age,
That then, in recompense of all thy cares
Thy child shall show respect to thy gray hairs.[39]

He never wrote a tribute to his father that we know of. He says almost nothing about him. But this is a powerful plea for fathers to love their children and give them special attention in their education. This is what he missed from the age of six onward.

Distrust the Certainties of Despair

What shall we learn from the life of William Cowper? The first lesson is this: We fortify ourselves against the dark hours of depression by cultivating a deep distrust of the certainties of despair. Despair is relentless in the certainties of his pessimism. But we have seen that Cowper is not consistent. Some years after his absolute statements of being cut off from God, he is again expressing some hope in being heard. His certainties were not sureties.

---

[39] Ibid., p. 236.

So it will always be with the deceptions of darkness. Let us now, while we have the light, cultivate distrust of the certainties of despair.

Love Your Children Dearly

The second lesson I see is that we should love our children deeply and keep communicating that love to them. And, unless some extraordinary call of God prevents it, let us keep them close to us and secure with us. John Newton, like William Cowper, lost his mother when he was six. But he did not lose his father in the same way. In spite of all the sin and misery of those early years of Newton's life, there was a father—even on the high seas, even setting a bad example in many ways. And who can say what deep roots of later health were preserved because of that one solid rock: a present father. But for Cowper the legacy of his father, who died when he was twenty-five, is marked by Cowper's total silence. Almost everything in his life that he valued he wrote poems about. But none for his father. Let us be there for our sons and daughters. We are a crucial link in their normal sexual and emotional development.

Despair Not of the Despairing

Third, may the Lord raise up many John Newtons among us, for the joy of our churches and for the survival of the William Cowpers in our midst. Newton remained Cowper's pastor and friend the rest of his life, writing and visiting again and again. He did not despair of the despairing. After one of these visits in 1788, Cowper wrote:

> I found those comforts in your visit, which have formerly sweetened all our interviews, in part restored. I knew you; knew you for the same shepherd who was sent to lead me out of the wilderness into the pasture where the Chief Shepherd feeds His flock, and felt my sentiments of affectionate friendship for you the same as ever. But one thing was still wanting, and that the crown of all. I shall find it in God's time, if it be not lost for ever.[40]

That is not utter hopelessness. And the reason it is not is because the shepherd had drawn near again. Those were the times when Cowper felt a ray of hope.

The Healthy Gift of Self-Forgetfulness

Fourth, in the very research and writing of this chapter I experienced something that may be a crucial lesson for those of us who are given to too much introspection and analysis. I devoted about three days—from waking until sleeping—to William Cowper, besides leisurely reading of his life and poetry before those three days. These days I was almost entirely outside myself as it were. Now and then I "came to" and became aware that I had been absorbed wholly in the life of another. But most of the time I was not self-conscious. I was not thinking about me at all. I was the one thinking, not the one thought about. This experience, when I "came to" and thought about it, seemed to me extremely healthy.

---

[40] Thomas, *William Cowper and the Eighteenth Century*, p. 356.

That is the way I experienced it. In other words, I felt best when I was not aware of being one who feels. I was feeling and thinking of something outside myself—the life of William Cowper.

I think this is the way most of life should be. Periodic self-examination is needed and wise and biblical. But for the most part, mental health is the use of the mind to focus on worthy reality outside ourselves. While I was a student at Wheaton College, a very wise and deep and happy teacher of literature, Clyde Kilby, showed us and taught us this path to health. Once he said, "I shall not demean my own uniqueness by envy of others. I shall stop boring into myself to discover what psychological or social categories I might belong to. Mostly I shall simply forget about myself and do my work."[41]

He had learned the deep significance of this outward-oriented self-forgetfulness from C. S. Lewis and drew our attention to it often. Mental health is, in great measure, the gift of self-forgetfulness. The reason is that introspection destroys what matters most to us—the authentic experience of great things outside ourselves. Lewis grasped this as well as anyone in the twentieth century:

> The enjoyment and the contemplation of our inner activities are incompatible. You cannot hope and also think about hoping at the same moment; for in hope we look to hope's object and we interrupt this by (so to speak) turning round to look at the hope itself. Of course the two activities can and do alternate with great rapidity. . . . The

---

[41] For this and nine other resolutions of Dr. Kilby, see John Piper, *The Pleasures of God: Meditations on God's Delight in Being God,* revised and expanded edition (Sisters, OR: Multnomah Publishers, 2000), p. 95.

surest means of disarming an anger or a lust was to turn your attention from the girl or the insult and start examining the passion itself. The surest way of spoiling a pleasure was to start examining your satisfaction. But if so, it followed that all introspection is in one respect misleading. In introspection we try to look "inside ourselves" and see what is going on. But nearly everything that was going on a moment before is stopped by the very act of our turning to look at it. Unfortunately this does not mean that introspection finds nothing. On the contrary, it finds precisely what is left behind by the suspension of all our normal activities; and what is left behind is mainly mental images and physical sensations. The great error is to mistake this mere sediment or track or byproduct for the activities themselves.[42]

Oh, the danger of too much pondering of our inner states! It distorts the bad and it suspends, or even destroys, the good.

You cannot study pleasure in the moment of the nuptial embrace, nor repentance while repenting, nor analyze the nature of humour while roaring with laughter. But when else can you really know these things? "If only my toothache would stop, I could write another chapter about pain." But once it stops, what do I know about pain?[43]

Self-forgetfulness in the contemplation of something great or the doing of something good is a gift from God. In the end, the harder you try to forget yourself, the more impossible it is. It

[42] C. S. Lewis, *Surprised by Joy: The Shape of My Early Life* (New York: Harcourt, Brace and World, Inc. 1955), pp. 218-219.

[43] Lewis, "Myth Became Fact," *God in the Dock* (Grand Rapids: William B. Eerdmans Publishing Co., 1970), pp. 65-66.

must be pursued indirectly. One great antidote to depression is simply to see what is really there in the world. Which is why Clyde Kilby resolved:

> I shall open my eyes and ears. Once every day I shall simply stare at a tree, a flower, a cloud, or a person. I shall not then be concerned at all to ask what they are, but simply be glad that they are. I shall joyfully allow them the mystery of what Lewis calls their "divine, magical, terrifying, and ecstatic" existence.[44]

Escape: The Path to Suicide

A fifth lesson I speak with some hesitation. We should be slow to judge the needs and possibilities of another person's mental health. But at least I suggest that Cowper would have benefited by less retreat and ease and contemplation and more engagement with suffering people who needed help. Gilbert Thomas says of Cowper's major poem *The Task* (more than one hundred pages), "The whole has one tendency: to discountenance the modern enthusiasm after a London life, and to recommend rural ease and leisure, as friendly to the cause of piety and virtue."[45] This is a remarkable contrast to what was brewing in William Carey's much healthier mind not far away. The last thing Carey wanted to do was to recommend rural ease and leisure! What was needed in the world was not people retreating to tea and lakes in order to be more virtuous than they would be in the London pubs. What was needed was people giving their lives away to rescue people

[44] Piper, *The Pleasures of God*, p. 95.
[45] Thomas, *William Cowper and the Eighteenth Century*, p. 197.

from the darkness of London and even more from the utter alienation of places like India.

Was Cowper cutting himself off from greater mental health by living a life of such continual leisure and distance from the world of need? He talks of his constant walks and religious conversations as though that were the aim of life. And his moralizing seems to be done from a safe distance from the London scenes. I cannot overlook the deep strain of escape in his life. I do not condemn him for this, because I simply do not know what a mind so fragile as his could endure.

Gilbert Thomas suggests, "That Cowper was an escapist, in the physical sense, may be true: his supersensitive nervous constitution demanded solitude."[46] Perhaps. But those of us who have the choice still in front of us would do well to ponder that neither health nor holiness are had by escape from perishing people. The path of love, no matter how dirty or dangerous, is the path to wholeness and heaven.

The Hope-Giving Fruit of Feeling Hopelessness

A sixth lesson from the life of William Cowper I have learned from how God seems to use it in the lives of others. Some years ago I presented an early version of this chapter as a Sunday evening message at Bethlehem Baptist Church. It proved to be one of the most encouraging things I had done in a long time. This bleak life was felt by many as hope-giving. There are no doubt different reasons for this in the cases of different people. But the lesson is surely that those

---

[46] Ibid., p. 321.

of us who teach and preach and want to encourage our people to press on in hope and faith must not limit ourselves to success stories. The tormented life of William Cowper had a hope-giving effect on my people. That is a very important lesson.

There is biblical warrant for this strange strategy of encouragement. For example, David, the king of Israel, speaks in Psalm 40:1-3 about his extended misery in "the pit of destruction" and "the miry clay." "I waited patiently for the LORD; and He inclined to me and heard my cry. He brought me up out of the pit of destruction, out of the miry clay." He does not tell us how long he "waited patiently." Hours? Days? Weeks? Months? The first point is that though he was there for an extended time, he did not curse God, but cried out. But the main point here is that people are helped by the testimony of his deliverance—not in spite of, but because of David's sharing in the miseries they all know. "He set my feet upon a rock making my footsteps firm. He put a new song in my mouth, a song of praise to our God; many will see and fear and will trust in the LORD." People feared God and put their trust in him because the king was in "the pit of destruction" and God heard his cry and delivered him. Who knows but that any misery we meet is not designed for such a painful path toward praise by other people?

Of course, one might object, "Yes, but David was delivered in this life and had a 'new song' put in his mouth. William Cowper didn't." That's probably true. I say "probably" because it may be that Cowper had new songs given to him again and again after repeated times of suicidal blackness. Whether he did in the end is doubtful. But this too is not unforeseen in the Bible.

When David says in Psalm 139:7, "Where can I go from Your

Spirit? Or where can I flee from Your presence?" his implied answer is "Nowhere." But his last place of retreat is the darkness of his own soul in a time of distress. "If I say, 'Surely the darkness will overwhelm me, and the light around me will be night,' even the darkness is not dark to You, and the night is as bright as the day. Darkness and light are alike to You" (Psalm 139:11-12). Notice that the issue here is not objective overwhelming darkness; it is David's *saying*, "Surely the darkness will overwhelm me." It is a subjective sense of darkness. It is despairing feelings. This sounds exactly like Cowper in the last days. "The light around me will be night." But to this, the answer is, "Even the darkness is not dark to You." What is dark to God's children—objectively and subjectively—is not dark to God.

The point is, there are stories in the Bible, in history, and in our own lives that do not appear to have happy endings of cheerfulness. These too are not without hope and are designed by God's sovereign and merciful wisdom for the hope of those who fear they are utterly alone in their misery. The principle is expressed by Paul in 1 Timothy 1:16, "For this reason I found mercy, so that in me as the foremost [sinner], Jesus Christ might demonstrate His perfect patience as an example for those who would believe in Him for eternal life." The examples of God's patience in history will not serve their saving and sustaining purposes if we do not tell the stories—like the story of William Cowper.

Never Cease to Sing the Gospel to the Deaf

One final, all-important lesson: Let us rehearse the mercies of Jesus often in the presence of discouraged people. Let us point them again and again to the blood of Jesus. These were the two things that brought Cowper to faith in 1764. Remember how he said that in John 11 he "saw so much benevolence, mercy, goodness, and sympathy with miserable men, in our Saviour's conduct, that I almost shed tears."[47] And remember how on the decisive day of awakening he said, "I saw the sufficiency of the atonement He had made, my pardon sealed in His blood, and all the fullness and completeness of His justification."[48]

In Cowper's most famous hymn, this is what he sings—the preciousness of the blood of Christ to the worst of sinners.

> *There is a fountain filled with blood*
> *Drawn from Emmanuel's veins;*
> *And sinners, plunged beneath that flood,*
> *Lose all their guilty stains.*
>
> *The dying thief rejoiced to see*
> *That fountain in his day;*
> *And there have I, as vile as he,*
> *Washed all my sins away.*
>
> *Dear dying Lamb, thy precious blood*
> *Shall never lose its power;*
> *Till all the ransomed church of God*
> *Be saved to sin no more.*
>
> *E'er since, by faith, I saw the stream*
> *Thy flowing wounds supply,*

---

[47] See note 18 above.
[48] See Introduction, note 29.

> *Redeeming love has been my theme,*
> *And shall be till I die.*[49]

Don't make your mercy to the downcast contingent on quick results. You cannot persuade a person that he is not reprobate if he is utterly persuaded that he is. He will tell you he is deaf. No matter. Keep soaking him in the "benevolence, mercy, goodness, and sympathy" of Jesus and "the sufficiency of the atonement" and "the fullness and completeness of [Christ's] justification." Yes, he may say that these are all wonderful in themselves, but that they do not belong to him. To this you say, "Doubt your despairing thoughts. Whence this great confidence you have in your damnation? A little skepticism is in order here. Who do you think you are"—perhaps you smile when you say this (but not lightly)—"making final declarations about your soul that lie hidden in the secrets of the Almighty? No. No. Renounce such confidence. If you have no ability for faith in the love of God for you, make no more such great pretenses to have such certainty of faith in your damnation. This is not yours to know. Rather, yours is to listen to Jesus." Then go on telling him the glories of Christ and his all-sufficient sacrifice for sin. Pray that in God's time these truths may yet be given the power to awaken hope and beget a spirit of adoption.

We have good reason to hope that if we make redeeming love our theme until we die, and if we promote the love and patience of John Newton in our own souls and in our churches, then the William Cowpers among us will not be given over to the enemy in the end.

---

[49] The original title in the *Olney Hymnal* was "Praise for the Fountain Opened." *The Poetical Works of William Cowper*, p. 280. There are three more verses than those cited here.

When I really enjoy God, I feel my desires of him the more

insatiable, and my thirstings after holiness the more

unquenchable. . . . Oh, for holiness! Oh, for more of God in

my soul! Oh, this pleasing pain! It makes my soul press after

God. . . . Oh, that I may feel this continual hunger, and not

be retarded, but rather animated by every "cluster from

Canaan," to reach forward in the narrow way, for the full

enjoyment and possession of the heavenly inheritance.

Oh, that I might never loiter on my heavenly journey!

DAVID BRAINERD
THE DIARY

3

"OH, THAT I MIGHT NEVER LOITER ON MY HEAVENLY JOURNEY!"

Misery and Mission in the Life of David Brainerd

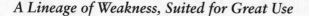

A Lineage of Weakness, Suited for Great Use

David Brainerd was born on April 20, 1718, in Haddam, Connecticut. That year John Wesley and Jonathan Edwards turned fourteen. Benjamin Franklin turned twelve and George Whitefield three. The Great Awakening was just over the horizon, and Brainerd would live through both waves of it in the mid-thirties and early forties of the eighteenth century, then die of tuberculosis in Jonathan Edwards's house at the age of twenty-nine on October 9, 1747.

Brainerd's father Hezekiah was a Connecticut legislator and died when David was nine years old. I have four sons of my own, and judging by their warm emotional attachment at that age, I think that might be the hardest year of all to lose a father. Hezekiah had been a rigorous Puritan with strong views of authority and strictness at home; and he pursued a very earnest devotion that included days of private fasting to promote spiritual welfare.[1]

---

[1] Jonathan Edwards, *The Life of David Brainerd*, ed. Norman Pettit, *The Works of Jonathan Edwards*, vol. 7 (New Haven, CT: Yale University Press, 1985), p. 33. All page numbers in the text refer to this volume, which contains not only Edwards's edition of Brainerd's *Diaries*, but also some journal extracts and an extensive introduction by Norman Pettit and related correspondence.

Brainerd was the sixth child and third son born to Hezekiah and Dorothy. After him came three more children. Dorothy had brought one little boy from a previous marriage, and so there were twelve of them in the home—but not for long. Five years after his father died at the age of forty-six, David's mother died just before he turned fourteen.

It seems there was an unusual strain of weakness and depression in the family. Not only did the parents die early, but also David's brother Nehemiah died at thirty-two, his brother Israel died at twenty-three, his sister Jerusha died at thirty-four, and he died at twenty-nine. In 1865 a descendant, Thomas Brainerd (in a biography of John Brainerd), said, "In the whole Brainerd family for two hundred years there has been a tendency to a morbid depression, akin to hypochondria" (p. 64).

So on top of having an austere father and suffering the loss of both parents as a sensitive child, David probably inherited some kind of physical tendency to depression. Whatever the cause, he suffered from the blackest dejection off and on throughout his short life. He says at the very beginning of his diary, "I was, I think, from my youth something sober and inclined rather to melancholy than the other extreme" (p. 101).

Religion with No True Grace in the Soul

When his mother died, he moved from Haddam across the Connecticut River to East Haddam to live with his married sister, Jerusha. He described his religion during these years as very careful and serious, but having no true grace—in other words, in the language of eighteenth-century Puritanism, unconverted, not a true Christian. When he turned nineteen, he inherited a farm and moved for a year a few miles west to Durham to try his hand at farming. But his heart was not in it. He longed for "a liberal education" (p. 103). In fact, Brainerd was a contemplative and a scholar from head to toe. If he hadn't been expelled from Yale, he may well have pursued a teaching or pastoral ministry instead of becoming a missionary to the Indians.

After a year on the farm he came back to East Haddam and began to prepare himself to enter Yale. This was the summer of 1738. He was twenty years old. During the year on the farm he had made a commitment to God to enter the ministry. But still he was not converted. He read the whole Bible twice that year and began to see more clearly that all his religion was legalistic and simply based on his own efforts. He had great quarreling with God within his soul. He rebelled against original sin and against the strictness of the divine law and against the sovereignty of God. He quarreled with the fact that there was nothing he could do in his own strength to commend himself to God (pp. 113-124).

He came to see that "all my good frames [i.e., devotional states] were but self-righteousness, not bottomed on a desire for the glory of God" (p. 103). "There was no more goodness in my praying than there would be in my paddling with my hands in the water . . . because [my prayers] were not performed from any love or regard to God. . . . I never once prayed for the glory of God" (p. 134). "I never once intended his honor and glory. . . . I had never once acted for God in all my devotions. . . . I used to charge them with sin . . . [because] of wanderings and vain thoughts . . . and not because I never had any regard in them to the glory of God" (p. 136).

"I Felt Myself in a New World"

But then the miracle happened, the day of his new birth. Half an hour before sunset at the age of twenty-one he was in a lonely place trying to pray.

> As I was walking in a dark thick grove, "unspeakable glory" seemed to open to the view and apprehension of my soul. . . . It was a new inward apprehension or view that I had of God; such as I never had before, nor anything that I had the least remembrance of it. So that I stood still and wondered and admired. . . . I had now no particular apprehension of any one person of the Trinity, either the Father, Son, or Holy Spirit, but it appeared to be divine glory and splendor that I then beheld. And my soul "rejoiced with joy unspeakable" to see such a God, such a glorious divine being, and I was inwardly pleased and satisfied that he should be God over all forever and ever. My soul was so captivated and delighted with the excellency, the loveliness and the greatness and other perfections of God that I was even swallowed up in him, at least to that degree that I had no thought, as I remember at first, about my own salvation or scarce that there was such a creature as I.
>
> Thus the Lord, I trust, brought me to a hearty desire to exalt him, to set him on the throne and to "seek first his Kingdom," i.e. principally and ultimately to aim at his honor and glory as the King and sovereign of the universe, which is the foundation of the religion Jesus Christ has taught. . . . I felt myself in a new world. . . . I wondered that all the world did not comply with this way of salvation entirely by the "righteousness of Christ." (pp. 138-140)

Jonathan Edwards wrote at the top of the manuscript of Brainerd's diary at this point, "Lord's Day, July 12th 1739 forever to be remembered by D. B." (p. 140). Brainerd was twenty-one years old. He had entered into an experience of God's grace that would ruin his educational career but rescue him again and again from despair.

Whittelsey "Has No More Grace Than a Chair"

Two months later he entered Yale to prepare for the ministry. It was a hard beginning. There was hazing by the upperclassmen, little spirituality, difficult studies, and he got measles and had to go home for several weeks during that first year.

The next year he was sent home because he was so sick he was spitting blood. So even at this early age he already had the tuberculosis he would die of seven years later. The amazing thing may not be that he died so early and accomplished so little, but that, being as sick as he was, he lived as long as he did and accomplished so much.

When he came back to Yale in November 1740, the spiritual climate was radically changed. George Whitefield had been there, and now many students were very serious about their faith, which suited Brainerd well. In fact, tensions were emerging between the awakened students and the seemingly less spiritual faculty and staff. In 1741, pastor-evangelists Gilbert Tennent, Ebenezer Pemberton, and James Davenport fanned the flames of discontent among the students with their fiery preaching.

Jonathan Edwards was invited to preach the commencement address in 1741 in the hopes that he would pour a little water on the fire and stand up for the faculty against the enthusiasm of the students. Some faculty had even been criticized as being unconverted. Edwards preached a sermon called "The Distinguishing Marks of a Work of the Spirit of God" and totally disappointed the faculty and staff. He argued that the work going on in the awakening of those days, and specifically among the students, was a real spiritual work in spite of the excesses.

That very morning it had been voted by the college trustees that "if any student of this College shall directly or indirectly say, that the Rector, either of the Trustees or tutors are hypocrites, carnal or unconverted men, he shall for the first offense make a public confession in the hall, and for the second offense be expelled" (p. 41). Edwards was clearly more sympathetic with the students than the college was. He even went so far as to say in his commencement address that afternoon, "it is no evidence that a work is not the work of God, if many that are subjects of it . . . are guilty of [so] great forwardness to censure others as unconverted" (p. 42).

Brainerd was in the crowd as Edwards spoke. One can't help but wonder whether Edwards later felt some responsibility for what happened to Brainerd in the next term. He was at the top of his class academically but was summarily expelled in early 1742 during his third year. He was overheard to say that one of the tutors, Chauncey Whittelsey, "has no more grace than a chair" and that he wondered why the Rector "did not drop down dead" for fining students for their evangelical zeal (pp. 42, 155).

The Lasting Fruit of Eight Wrong Words

This expulsion wounded Brainerd very deeply. He tried again and again in the next several years to make things right.

Numerous people came to his aid, but all to no avail. God had another plan for Brainerd. Instead of a quiet six years in the pastorate or lecture hall followed by death and little historical impact for Christ's kingdom, God meant to drive him into the wilderness that he might suffer for his sake and have an incalculable influence on the history of missions.

Before the way was cut off for him to the pastorate, Brainerd had no thought of being a missionary to the Indians. But now he had to rethink his whole life. There was a law, recently passed, that no established minister could be installed in Connecticut who had not graduated from Harvard, Yale, or a European university (p. 52). So Brainerd felt cut off from his life calling.

There is a tremendous lesson here. God is at work for the glory of his name and the good of his church even when the good intentions of his servants fail—even when that failing is owing to sin or carelessness. One careless word, spoken in haste, and Brainerd's life seemed to fall apart before his eyes. But God knew better, and Brainerd came to accept it. In fact, I am tempted to speculate whether the modern missionary movement, which was so repeatedly inspired by Brainerd's missionary life, would have happened if David Brainerd had not been expelled from Yale and cut off from his hopes to serve God in the pastorate! But God alone knows the "would-have-been's" of history (Matthew 11:21).

Lose the Good and Gain the Best

In the summer of 1742, a group of ministers (called New Lights) sympathetic to the Great Awakening licensed Brainerd to preach.

Jonathan Dickinson, the leading Presbyterian in New Jersey, took an interest in Brainerd and tried to get him reinstated in Yale. When that failed, the suggestion was made that Brainerd become a missionary to the Indians under the sponsorship of the Commissioners of the Society in Scotland for Propagating Christian Knowledge. Dickinson was one of those Commissioners. On November 25, 1742, Brainerd was examined for his fitness for the work and was appointed as a missionary to the Indians (p. 188).

He spent the winter serving a church on Long Island so that he could enter the wilderness in the spring. His first assignment was to the Housatonic Indians at Kaunaumeek, about twenty miles northwest of Stockbridge, Massachusetts, where Jonathan Edwards would eventually serve as a missionary to the Indians. He arrived on April 1, 1743, and preached for one year, using an interpreter and trying to learn the language from John Sergeant, the veteran missionary at Stockbridge (p. 228). While here he was able to start a school for Indian children and translate some of the Psalms (p. 61).

Then came a reassignment to go to the Indians along the Delaware River in Pennsylvania. On May 1, 1744, he left Kaunaumeek and settled in the Forks of the Delaware River, northeast of Bethlehem, Pennsylvania. At the end of the month he rode to Newark, New Jersey, to be examined by the Newark Presbytery and was ordained on June 11, 1744 (pp. 251-252).

At Last God Moved with Amazing Power

He preached to the Indians at the Forks of the Delaware for one year. But on June 19, 1745, he made his first preaching tour to the Indians at Crossweeksung, New Jersey. This was the place where God moved in amazing power and brought awakening and blessing to the Indians. Within a year there were 130 persons in his growing assembly of believers (p. 376). The whole, newly-converted Christian community moved from Crossweeksung to Cranberry in May, 1746, to have their own land and village. Brainerd stayed with these Indians until he was too sick to minister, and in November 1746 he left Cranberry to spend four months trying to recuperate in Elizabethtown at the house of Jonathan Dickinson.

On March 20, 1747, he made one last visit to his Indian friends and then rode to the house of Jonathan Edwards in Northampton, Massachusetts, arriving May 28, 1747. He made one trip to Boston during the summer and then returned and died of tuberculosis in Edwards's house on October 9, 1747.

One Short Life

It was a short life—twenty-nine years, five months, and nineteen days. And only eight of those years as a believer. Only four as a missionary. Why has Brainerd's life made the impact that it has? One obvious reason is that Jonathan Edwards took the *Diaries* and published them as a *Life of Brainerd* in 1749. But why has this book never been out of print? Why did John Wesley say, "Let every preacher read carefully over the *Life of David Brainerd*" (p. 3)? Why was it written of Henry Martyn (missionary to India and Persia) that "perusing the life of David Brainerd, his soul was filled with a holy emulation of that extraordinary man; and after deep consideration and fervent prayer, he was at length fixed in a resolution to imitate his example"?[2] Why did William Carey regard Edwards's *Life of Brainerd* as precious and holy? Why did Robert Morrison and Robert McCheyne of Scotland and John Mills of America and Fredrick Schwartz of Germany and David Livingstone of England and Andrew Murray of South Africa and Jim Elliot of twentieth-century America look upon Brainerd with a kind of awe and draw power from him as countless others have (p. 4)?

Gideon Hawley, another missionary protégé of Jonathan Edwards, spoke for hundreds when he wrote in 1753 about his struggles as a missionary: "I need, greatly need, something more than humane [human or natural] to support me. I read my Bible and Mr. Brainerd's *Life*, the only books I brought with me, and from them have a little support" (p. 3).

Why has this life had such a remarkable influence? Or perhaps I should pose a more modest and manageable question: Why does it have such an impact on me? How has it helped me to press on in the ministry and to strive for holiness and divine power and fruitfulness in my life?

The answer is that Brainerd's life is a vivid, powerful testimony to the truth that God can and does use weak, sick, discouraged, beat-down, lonely, struggling saints who cry to him day and night to accomplish amazing things for his glory. There is great fruit in their afflictions. To illustrate this we will look first at Brainerd's struggles, then at how he responded to them, and finally at how God used him with all his weaknesses.

---

[2] "Brainerd, David," *Religious Encyclopaedia*, vol. 1, Philip Schaff, ed. (New York: The Christian Literature Company, 1888), p. 320.

Brainerd Struggled with Almost Constant Sickness

He had to drop out of college for some weeks because he had begun to cough up blood in 1740. In May 1744 he wrote, "Rode several hours in the rain through the howling wilderness, although I was so disordered in body that little or nothing but blood came from me" (p. 247).

Now and again he would write something like, "In the afternoon my pain increased exceedingly; and was obliged to betake myself to bed. . . . Was sometimes almost bereaved of the exercise of my reason by the extremity of pain" (p. 253). In August of 1746 he wrote, "Having lain in cold sweat all night, I coughed much bloody matter this morning, and was under great disorder of body, and not a little melancholy" (p. 420). In September he wrote, "Exercised with a violent cough and a considerable fever; had no appetite to any kind of food; and frequently brought up what I ate, as soon as it was down; and oftentimes had little rest in my bed, by reason of pains in my breast and back: was able, however, to ride over to my people, about two miles, every day, and take some care of those who were then at work upon a small house for me to reside in amongst the Indians" (p. 430).

In May 1747 at Jonathan Edwards's house, the doctors told him that he had incurable consumption and did not have long to live (p. 447). In the last couple of months of his life the suffering was incredible. September 24: "In the greatest distress that ever I endured having an uncommon kind of hiccough; which either strangled me or threw me into a straining to vomit" (p. 469). Edwards comments that in the week before Brainerd died, "He told me it was impossible for any to conceive of the distress he felt in his breast. He manifested much concern lest he should dishonor God by impatience under his extreme agony; which was such that he said the thought of enduring it one minute longer was almost insupportable." The night before he died he said to those around him that "it was another thing to die than people imagined" (pp. 475-476).

What strikes the reader of these diaries is not just the severity of Brainerd's suffering in the days before antibiotics and painkillers, but especially how relentless the sickness was. It was almost always there. And yet he pressed on with his work.

Brainerd Struggled with Recurring Depression

Brainerd came to understand more fully from his own experience the difference between spiritual desertion and the disease of melancholy. So his later judgments about his own spiritual condition are probably more careful than the earlier ones. But however one assesses his psychological condition, he was tormented again and again with the most desperate discouragements. And the marvel is that he survived and kept going at all.

Brainerd said he had been this way from his youth (p. 101). But he said that there was a difference between the depression he suffered before and after his conversion. After his conversion there seemed to be a rock of electing love under him that supported him, so that in his darkest times he could still affirm the truth and goodness of God, even though he couldn't sense it for a season (pp. 93, 141, 165, 278).

But even so, it was bad enough. Often his distress was owing to the hatred of his own remaining sinfulness. Thursday,

November 4, 1942: "'Tis distressing to feel in my soul that hell of corruption which still remains in me" (p. 185). Sometimes this sense of unworthiness was so intense that he felt cut off from the presence of God. January 23, 1743: "Scarce ever felt myself so unfit to exist, as now: I saw I was not worthy of a place among the Indians, where I am going. . . . None knows, but those that feel it, what the soul endures that is sensibly shut out from the presence of God: Alas, 'tis more bitter than death!" (pp. 195-196).

He often called his depression a kind of death. There are at least twenty-two places in the diary where he longed for death as a freedom from his misery. For example, Sunday, February 3, 1745: "My soul remembered 'the wormwood and the gall' (I might almost say hell) of Friday last; and I was greatly afraid I should be obliged again to drink of that 'cup of trembling,' which was inconceivably more bitter than death, and made me long for the grave more, unspeakably more, than for hid treasures" (p. 285). Sunday, December 16, 1744: "Was so overwhelmed with dejection that I knew not how to live: I longed for death exceedingly: My soul was 'sunk in deep waters,' and 'the floods' were ready to 'drown me': I was so much oppressed that my soul was in a kind of horror" (p. 278).

Perhaps the worse mental condition of all was the disappearance of all capacity to fear or to love at all. Some passages that reveal these times are so bleak that Jonathan Edwards left them out of his *Life*. We know this because there are thirty-six pages of Brainerd's diary in his own hand preserved at the Beineke Library at Yale University that can be compared with the way Edwards edited these pages (pp. 79, 100-153). Here is one such section that shows an aspect of Brainerd's depression that is classic in its numbness against any feeling at all.

I felt something like a criminal at the bar waiting for his sentence, excepting this, I felt but little concern which way my case went, for the fear of hell was almost, if not entirely, taken away from me. I had the greatest certainty that my state was forever unalterable by anything that I could do, and wondered and was almost astonished that I had never been sensible of it before because it [*sic,* I] had now the clearest demonstration of it. And in this case I felt neither love to God, or desire of heaven as I used to think I did. Neither fear of hell, or love to the present world. Indeed I had rather be, or suffer anything than return to my former course of carelessness. I thought my convictions were all gone and that seemed dreadful. But I thought I could but go to hell, and that I had no sense of, nor could make it appear dreadful as formerly. Indeed I seemed to feel wholly destitute of any happiness or hopes and expectations of happiness either in the present or coming world, and yet felt no considerable degree of misery sensibly though I felt indeed something so far bordering on despair of any satisfying good that it appeared almost as comfortable to think of being annihilated as anything that I then knew of, though I can truly say I was not willing for that neither. My whole soul was unspeakably bewildered and lost in myself and I knew of nothing that seemed likely to make me happy, in case I could with the greatest ease have obtained the best good that I had any conception of. And being that lost I became a suitable object for the compassion of Jesus Christ to be set upon, since he came "to seek and to save that which is lost." (Luke 19:10) (pp. 131-133)

Only in retrospect did he see himself as a "suitable object

for the compassion of Jesus Christ." But in the hour of darkness there was no sense of hope or love or fear. This is the most fearful side of depression, since the natural restraints on suicide begin to vanish. But, unlike William Cowper, Brainerd was spared the suicidal drive. His wishes for death were all restrained within the bounds of the biblical truth, "The LORD gave and the LORD has taken away" (Job 1:21). He wishes for death many times, but only that God would take him (pp. 172, 183, 187, 215, 249, for example).

It caused him compounded misery when he thought how much his mental distress hindered his ministry and his devotion. Wednesday, March 9, 1743: "Rode 16 miles to Montauk, and had some inward sweetness on the road, but something of flatness and deadness after I came there and had seen the Indians: I withdrew and endeavored to pray, but found myself awfully deserted and left, and had an afflicting sense of my vileness and meanness" (p. 199).

At times he was simply immobilized by the distresses and couldn't function anymore. Tuesday, September 2, 1746: "Was scarce ever more confounded with a sense of my own unfruitfulness and unfitness of my work, than now. Oh, what a dead, heartless, barren, unprofitable wretch did I now see myself to be! My spirits were so low, and my bodily strength so wasted, that I could do nothing at all. At length, being much overdone, lay down on a buffalo skin; but sweat much of the whole night" (pp. 423ff.).

It is simply amazing how often Brainerd pressed on with the practical necessities of his work in the face of these waves of discouragement. This has no doubt endeared him to many missionaries who know firsthand the kinds of pain he endured.

Brainerd Struggled with Loneliness

He tells of having to endure the profane talk of two strangers one night in April 1743 and says, "Oh, I longed that some dear Christian knew my distress!" (p. 204). A month later he says, "Most of the talk I hear is either Highland Scotch or Indian. I have no fellow Christian to whom I might unbosom myself and lay open my spiritual sorrows, and with whom I might take sweet counsel in conversation about heavenly things, and join in social prayer" (p. 207). This misery made him sometimes shrink back from going off on another venture. Tuesday, May 8, 1744: "My heart sometimes was ready to sink with the thoughts of my work, and going alone in the wilderness, I knew not where" (p. 248).

In December 1745, he wrote a letter to his friend Eleazar Wheelock and said, "I doubt not by that time you have read my journal through you'll be more sensible of the need I stand in of a companion in travel than ever you was [sic] before" (p. 584). But he didn't just want any kind of person, of course. He wanted a soul companion. Many of us can empathize with him when he says, "There are many with whom I can talk about religion: but alas, I find few with whom I can talk religion itself: But, blessed be the Lord, there are some that love to feed on the kernel rather than the shell" (p. 292).

But Brainerd was alone in his ministry to the end. During the last nineteen weeks of his life, Jerusha Edwards, Jonathan Edwards's seventeen-year-old daughter, was his nurse, and many speculate that there was deep (even romantic) love between them. But in the wilderness and in the ministry he was alone and could only pour out his soul to God. And God bore him and kept him going.

Brainerd Struggled with Immense External Hardships

He describes his first mission station at Kaunaumeek in May 1743: "I live poorly with regard to the comforts of life: most of my diet consists of boiled corn, hasty pudding, etc. I lodge on a bundle of straw, and my labor is hard and extremely difficult; and I have little experience of success to comfort me" (p. 207). In August he says, "In this weak state of body, [I] was not a little distressed for want of suitable food. Had no bread, nor could I get any. I am forced to go or send ten or fifteen miles for all the bread I eat; and sometimes 'tis moldy and sour before I eat it, if I get any considerable quantity. . . . But through divine goodness I had some Indian meal, of which I made little cakes and fried them. Yet felt contented with my circumstances, and sweetly resigned to God" (pp. 213-214).

He says that he was frequently lost in the woods and was exposed to cold and hunger (p. 222). He speaks of his horse being stolen or being poisoned or having a broken leg (pp. 294, 339). He tells about how the smoke from a fireplace would often make the room intolerable to his lungs and he would have to go out into the cold to get his breath, and then could not sleep through the night (p. 422).

But the battle with external hardships, as great as they were, was not his worst struggle. He had an amazing resignation and even rest, it seems, in many of these circumstances. He knew where they fit in his biblical approach to life:

Such fatigues and hardship as these serve to wean me more from the earth; and, I trust, will make heaven the sweeter. Formerly, when I was thus exposed to cold, rain, etc., I was ready to please myself with the thoughts of enjoying a comfortable house, a warm fire, and other outward comforts; but now these have less place in my heart (through the grace of God) and my eye is more to God for comfort. In this world I expect tribulation; and it does not now, as formerly, appear strange to me; I don't in such seasons of difficulty flatter myself that it will be better hereafter; but rather think how much worse it might be; how much greater trials others of God's children have endured; and how much greater are yet perhaps reserved for me. Blessed be God that he makes [is] the comfort to me, under my sharpest trials; and scarce ever lets these thoughts be attended with terror or melancholy; but they are attended frequently with great joy. (p. 274)

So in spite of the terrible external hardships that Brainerd knew, he pressed on and even flourished under these tribulations that led to the weight of glory in the kingdom of God.

Brainerd Struggled with a Bleak Outlook on Nature

We will forgive him for this quickly because few of us have suffered physically what he suffered or endured the hardships he did in the wilderness. It is hard to relish the beauty of a rose when you are coughing up blood.

But we have to see this as part of Brainerd's struggle because an eye for beauty instead of bleakness might have lightened some of his load. Edwards extolled Brainerd for not being a person of "warm imagination" (p. 93). This was a virtue for Edwards because it meant that Brainerd was free from what he called religious "enthusiasm"—the intensity of religious emotion based on sudden impressions and sights in the imagination rather than on spiritual apprehension of God's moral perfections. So Edwards applauded Brainerd for not having "strong and lively images formed in his imagination" (p. 93).

But there is a costly downside to an unimaginative mind. In Brainerd's case it meant that he seemed to see nothing in nature but a "howling wilderness" and a bleak enemy. There was nothing in his diaries like the transports of Jonathan Edwards as he walked in the woods and saw images of divine glory and echoes of God's excellence everywhere. In his *Personal Narrative*, Edwards tells us of several early experiences not long after his teenage awakening that reveal the kind of seeing heart he had in regard to the beauties of nature.

I walked abroad alone, in a solitary place in my father's pasture, for contemplation. And as I was walking there, and looking up on the sky and clouds, there came into my mind so sweet a sense of the glorious *majesty* and *grace* of God, that I know not how to express. I seemed to see them both in a sweet conjunction; majesty and meekness joined together: it was a sweet and gentle, and holy majesty; and also a majestic meekness; an awful sweetness; a high, and great, and holy gentleness.

The appearance of everything was altered; there seemed to be, as it were, a calm, sweet cast, or appearance of divine glory, in almost everything. God's excellency, his wisdom, his purity and love, seemed to appear in everything; in the sun, and moon, and stars; in the clouds and blue sky; in the grass, flowers, trees; in the water, and all nature; which used greatly to fix my mind. I often used to sit and view the moon for a long time; and in the day, spent much time in viewing the clouds and sky, to behold the sweet glory of God in these things; in the meantime, singing forth, with a low voice, my contemplations of the Creator and Redeemer.[3]

Norman Pettit is right, it seems to me, when he says,

Where Edwards saw mountains and waste places as the setting for divine disclosure, Brainerd saw only a "howling desert." Where Edwards could take spiritual delight "in the sun, moon, and stars; in the clouds, and blue sky; in the grass, flowers, trees," Brainerd never mentioned natural beauty. In contrast to Edwards' joy in summer is Brainerd's fear of winter. (p. 23)

Brainerd never mentioned an attractive landscape or sunset. He did at one place say he had discovered the need for diversions in his labor for the sake of maximizing his usefulness (p. 292). But he never once described such a diversion or any impact that it had on him.

It is a sad thing that Brainerd was blinded (perhaps by his own suffering[4]) to one of God's antidotes to depression. Charles Spurgeon, the great British preacher and pastor from the late

[3] Jonathan Edwards, *Personal Narrative*, in *Jonathan Edwards: Selections*, Clarence H. Faust and Thomas H. Johnson, eds. (New York: Hill and Wang, 1962), pp. 60-61.

[4] Clyde Kilby laments Brainerd's "defection from Scripture itself" in his "seeming total disregard of the heavens and the earth as the handiwork of God. In the more than six hundred pages of the *Diary* and *Journal* there are fewer than a half-dozen instances in which the very suggestion of any regard for natural beauty occurs. . . . So far as the record shows, never once did a bird's song pierce his ear as it did King Solomon's and never once did Brainerd feel, like King David, the tenderness of still waters and green pastures. Never once is it evident that, like Christ, he observed the lilies of the field." And Kilby will not allow that Brainerd's ill health is a sufficient explanation for this defect: "To be sure, Brainerd's experience was not that of a man who goes for an outing in nature. He knew what it meant to be lost at night in the forest (but for that matter so did John Wesley) and to hear the wolves howling around him. The wilderness was for him an enemy to be overcome. Brainerd's antipathy to mountains cannot be accounted for on the ground of his ill health, for he had unusually good health on his first visit to the frontier over the Blue Mountains and through the lovely Lehigh Gap, yet it was nothing more than 'a hideous and howling wilderness' to him" ("David Brainerd: Knight of the Grail," in *Heroic Colonial Christians*, Russell T. Hitt, ed. [Philadelphia: J. B. Lippincott Company, 1966], pp. 182-183).

1800s who knew his own share of discouragement and depression, described this God-given remedy for melancholy that Brainerd seemed unable to taste:

> Nature . . . is calling him to health and beckoning him to joy. He who forgets the humming of the bees among the heather, the cooing of the wood-pigeons in the forest, the song of birds in the woods, the rippling of rills among the rushes, and the sighing of the wind among the pines, needs not wonder if his heart forgets to sing and his soul grows heavy. A day's breathing of fresh air upon the hills, or a few hours' ramble in the beech woods' umbrageous calm, would sweep the cobwebs out of the brain of scores of our toiling ministers who are not but half alive. A mouthful of sea air, or a stiff walk in the wind's face, would not give grace to the soul, but it would yield oxygen to the body, which is next best. . . . For lack of opportunity, or inclination, these great remedies are neglected, and the student becomes a self-immolated victim.[5]

I say again we will forgive Brainerd quickly for not drawing strength and refreshment from God's gallery of joy, because his suffering made it so hard for him to see. But we must make every effort not to succumb with him here. Spurgeon and Edwards are the models for us on spiritual uses of nature. And, of course, an even greater authority said, "Consider the lilies" (Matthew 6:28, KJV).

---

[5] Charles Spurgeon, *Lectures to My Students* (Grand Rapids, MI: Zondervan Publishing House, 1972), p. 158.

Brainerd Struggled to Love the Indians

If love is known by sacrifice, then Brainerd loved immensely. But if it is also known by heartfelt compassion, then Brainerd struggled to love more than he did. Sometimes he was melted with love. September 18, 1742: "Felt some compassion for souls, and mourned I had no more. I feel much more kindness, meekness, gentleness and love towards all mankind, than ever" (p. 181). December 26, 1742: "Felt much sweetness and tenderness in prayer, especially my whole soul seemed to love my worst enemies, and was enabled to pray for those that are strangers and enemies to God with a great degree of softness and pathetic fervor" (p. 193). Tuesday, July 2, 1745: "Felt my heart drawn out after God in prayer, almost all the forenoon; especially while riding. And in the evening, could not help crying to God for those poor Indians; and after I went to bed my heart continued to go out to God for them, till I dropped asleep. Oh, 'Blessed be God that I may pray!'" (p. 302).

But other times he seemed empty of affection or compassion for their souls. He expresses guilt that he should preach to immortal souls with no more ardency and so little desire for their salvation (p. 235). His compassion could simply go flat. November 2, 1744: "About noon, rode up to the Indians; and while going, could feel no desires for them, and even dreaded to say anything to 'em" (p. 272). So Brainerd struggled with the rise and fall of love in his own heart. He loved, but longed to love so much more.

Brainerd Struggled to Stay True to His Calling

Even though Brainerd's expulsion from Yale initially hindered his entering the pastorate and turned him to consider the missionary career, the missionary call he felt from the Lord in this was not abandoned when other opportunities for the pastorate finally did come along. There were several opportunities for him to have a much easier life in the settled life of the parish minister.

The church at Millington, near his hometown of Haddam, called him in March 1744, and he describes the call as a great care and burden. He turned it down and prayed that the Lord would send laborers to his vineyard (p. 244). The church at East Hampton on Long Island called him too. Jonathan Edwards called this "the fairest, pleasantest town on the whole island, and one of its largest and most wealthy parishes" (p. 245, note 8). Brainerd wrote on Thursday, April 5: "Resolved to go on still with the Indian affair, if divine providence permitted; although before felt some inclination to go to East Hampton, where I was solicited to go" (p. 245).

There were other opportunities too. But each time the struggle was resolved with this sense of burden and call: "[I] could have no freedom in the thought of any other circumstances or business in life: All my desire was the conversion of the heathen, and all my hope was in God: God does not suffer me to please or comfort myself with hopes of seeing friends, returning to my dear acquaintance, and enjoying worldly comforts" (p. 263). So the struggle was obviously there, but he was held to his post by a readiness to suffer and a passion to see the kingdom of Christ spread among the Indians.

A Passion to Finish Well

We turn now to how Brainerd responded to these struggles. What we are struck with immediately is that he pressed on. One of the main reasons Brainerd's life has such powerful effects on people is that in spite of all his struggles he never gave up his faith or his ministry. He was consumed with a passion to finish his race, and honor his Master, and spread the kingdom, and advance in personal holiness. It was this unswerving allegiance to the cause of Christ that makes the bleakness of his life glow with glory so that we can understand Henry Martyn when he wrote, as a student in Cambridge in 1802, "I long to be like him!" (p. 4).

There is something that captures the soul when we see a man of single-minded passion, persevering against all odds, finishing his course no matter the cost. The spirit of Jesus, when he set his face like flint to go to Jerusalem (Luke 9:51, 53), runs through the generations of all his most inspiring followers. Does not our spine tingle with longing to be radically devoted to Christ when we read, for example, Paul's determined purpose that puts submission above security: "I do not account my life of any value nor as precious to myself, if only I may accomplish my course and the ministry which I received from the Lord Jesus, to testify to the gospel of the grace of God!" (Acts 20:24, RSV). Single-minded devotion, which makes all else die away, captures the heart and makes us long, with Thomas, to follow no matter what: "Let us also go, so that we may die with Him" (John 11:16).

Clyde Kilby attributed Brainerd's influence to this kind of inspiration.

It is not Brainerd's accomplishments as a missionary, significant as they were, that have perpetuated his influence. It certainly is not his perturbations of spirit or his sense of vileness or his flagellation "complex" or his morbidity. I venture to say that it is not even his diary so much as the *idea* back of all which eventuated in molding the man. In our timidity and our shoddy opportunism we are always stirred when a man appears on the horizon willing to stake his all on a conviction.[6]

A Kind of "Pleasing Pain"

Brainerd's conviction was that no aspiration on earth surpassed the supreme purpose to savor and spread the reign of Christ in his own personal holiness and the conversion of the Indians for the glory of God. He called his passion for more holiness and more usefulness a kind of "pleasing pain." "When I really enjoy God, I feel my desires of him the more insatiable, and my thirstings after holiness the more unquenchable. . . . Oh, for holiness! Oh, for more of God in my soul! Oh, this pleasing pain! It makes my soul press after God. . . . Oh, that I might never loiter on my heavenly journey!" (p. 186).

He was gripped by the apostolic admonition: "Walk circumspectly . . . redeeming the time, because the days are evil" (Ephesians 5:15-16, KJV). He embodied the counsel: "Let us not be weary in well doing, for in due season we shall reap, if we faint not" (Galatians 6:9, KJV). He strove to be, as Paul says, "abounding in the work of the Lord" (1 Corinthians 15:58). April

---

[6] Kilby, "David Brainerd: Knight of the Grail," p. 202.

17, 1747: "O I longed to fill the remaining moments all for God! Though my body was so feeble, and wearied with preaching and much private conversation, yet I wanted to sit up all night to do something for God. To God the giver of these refreshments, be glory forever and ever; Amen" (p. 246). February 21, 1746: "My soul was refreshed and comforted, and I could not but bless God, who had enabled me in some good measure to be faithful in the day past. Oh, how sweet it is to be spent and worn out for God!" (p. 366).

"In Prayer . . . Ineffable Comforts into My Soul"

Among all the means that Brainerd used for pursuing greater and greater holiness and usefulness, prayer and fasting stand out above all. We read of him spending whole days in prayer. Wednesday, June 30, 1742: "Spent almost the whole day in prayer incessantly" (p. 172). Sometimes he set aside as many as six periods in the day to pray: "Blessed be God, I had much freedom five or six times in the day, in prayer and praise, and felt a weighty concern upon my spirit for the salvation of those precious souls and the enlargement of the Redeemer's kingdom among them" (p. 280).

Sometimes he would seek out a family or friend to pray with. He prayed for his own sanctification. He prayed for the conversion and purity of his Indians. He prayed for the advancement of the kingdom of Christ around the world and especially in America. Sometimes the spirit of prayer would hold him so deeply that he could scarcely stop.

These were some of the sweetest times for Brainerd, and he writes of them in ways that make the saint's heart hunger for God:

Retired pretty early for secret devotions; and in prayer God was pleased to pour such ineffable comforts into my soul that I could do nothing for some time but say over and over, "O my sweet Saviour! O my sweet Saviour!" "Whom have I in heaven but thee? and there is none upon earth, that I desire beside thee" [Ps. 73:25]. If I had a thousand lives my soul would gladly have laid 'em all down at once to have been with Christ. My soul never enjoyed so much of heaven before. 'Twas the most refined and most spiritual season of communion with God I ever yet felt. I never felt so great a degree of resignation in my life. (pp. 164-165)

Once, visiting in a home with friends in May 1746, he got alone to pray:

I continued wrestling with God in prayer for my dear little flock here; and more especially for the Indians elsewhere; as well as for dear friends in one place and another; till it was bed time and I feared I should hinder the family, etc. But oh, with what reluctancy did I find myself obliged to consume time in sleep! (p. 402)

A Birthday with No Cake, No Food

And along with prayer Brainerd pursued holiness and usefulness with fasting. Again and again in his diary he tells of days spent in fasting. One of the most remarkable, in view of how most of us celebrate our birthdays, is the fast on his twenty-fifth birthday:

Wednesday, April 20. Set apart this day for fasting and prayer, to bow my soul before God for the bestowment of divine grace; especially that all my spiritual afflictions and inward distresses might be sanctified to my soul. And endeavored also to remember the goodness of God to me the year past, this day being my birthday. Having obtained help of God, I have hitherto lived and am now arrived at the age of twenty-five years. My soul was pained to think of my barrenness and deadness; that I have lived so little to the glory of the eternal God. I spent the day in the woods alone, and there poured out my complaint to God. Oh, that God would enable me to live to His glory for the future! (p. 205)

He fasted for guidance when he was perplexed about the next steps of his ministry. Monday, April 19, 1742: "I set apart this day for fasting and prayer to God for his grace, especially to prepare me for the work of the ministry, to give me divine aid and direction in my preparations for that great work, and in his own time to 'Send me into his harvest' [Matthew 9:38; Luke 10:2]" (p. 162). And he fasted simply with the hope of making greater advances in his own spiritual life and holiness. Thursday, February 9, 1744: "Observed this day as a day of fasting and prayer, entreating of God to bestow upon me his blessing and grace; especially to enable me to live a life of mortification to the world, as well as of resignation and patience" (p. 238).

When he was dying in Jonathan Edwards's house, he urged young ministers who came to see him to engage in frequent days of private prayer and fasting because of how useful it was (p. 473). Edwards himself said, "Among all the many days [Brainerd] spent in secret fasting and prayer and that he gives an account of in his diary, there is scarce an instance of one but what was either attended or soon followed with apparent success and a remarkable blessing in special incomes and consolations of God's Spirit; and very often before the day was ended" (p. 531).

"Studied Closely, Till I Felt My Bodily Strength Fail"

Along with prayer and fasting, Brainerd bought up the time with study and mingled all three of these together. December 20, 1745: "I spent much of the day in writing; but was enabled to intermix prayer with my studies" (p. 280). January 7, 1744: "Spent this day in seriousness, with steadfast resolutions for God and a life of mortification. Studied closely, till I felt my bodily strength fail" (p. 234). December 20, 1742: "Spent this day in prayer, reading and writing; and enjoyed some assistance, especially in correcting some thoughts on a certain subject" (p. 192).

He was constantly writing and thinking about theological things. That's why we have the *Diaries* and *Journal*! But there was more. We frequently read things like, "Was most of the day employed in writing on a divine subject. Was frequent in prayer" (p. 240). "I spent most of the time in writing on a sweet divine subject" (p. 284). "Was engaged in writing again almost the whole day" (p. 287). "Rose early and wrote by candlelight some considerable time; spent most of the day in writing" (p. 344). "Towards night, enjoyed some of the clearest thoughts on a divine subject . . . that ever I remember to have had upon any subject whatsoever; and spent two or three hours in writing them" (p. 359).

Writing on a "Divine Subject . . . So Sweet an Entertainment"

Why all this writing? There are at least two reasons why Brainerd and why I and many others count writing an essential part of our spiritual life—not just ministerial life, but spiritual life. First, it brings clarity to the mind about great matters that we are reading or thinking about. Second, it intensifies the affections that are kindled by the clear and solid sight of great truth. Brainerd mentions both of these motivations in the entry from February 1, 1746:

> Towards night, enjoyed some of the clearest thoughts on a divine subject (viz., that treated of 1 Corinthians 15:13-16) that ever I remember to have had upon any subject whatsoever; and spent two or three hours in writing them. I was refreshed with the intenseness: My mind was so engaged in these meditations I could scarcely turn it to anything else; and indeed I could not be willing to part with so sweet an entertainment. (p. 359)

"An Habitual Vision of Greatness"

Just at this point Brainerd is so needed by our breezy culture. His meditations and writing were continually about "divine subjects." His thought and writing were marked by what he called "intenseness." Our day is marked, on the contrary, by small subjects and casual treatments. Richard Foster lamented this in 1996 with these words:

I am concerned that our reading and our writing is gravitating to the lowest common denominator so completely that the great themes of majesty and nobility and felicity are made to seem trite, puny, pedestrian. . . . In reality I am concerned about the state of the soul in the midst of all the cheap sensory overload going on today. You see, without what Alfred North Whitehead called "an habitual vision of greatness," our soul will shrivel up and lose the capacity for beauty and mystery and transcendence. . . . In this day and age having nothing at all to say does not disqualify a person from writing a book. The sad truth is that many authors simply have never learned to reflect substantively on anything.[7]

Brainerd's prayer, his meditation, his writing, and his whole life are one sustained indictment of our trivial time and culture—even much Christian culture. So much was at stake for Brainerd! He exemplified what Foster exhorted: "Give sustained attention to the great themes of the human spirit—life and death, transcendence, the problem of evil, the human predicament, the greatness of rightness, and much more."[8] Brainerd did this, not out of concern for sustaining the greatness of his own soul, but out of passion for the greatness of God in Christ, and the tragedy of unreached Indians entering eternity without a saving knowledge of this God. Therefore his life was one long agonizing strain to be "redeeming . . . the time" (Ephesians 5:16, KJV) and "not be weary in well doing" (Galatians 6:9, KJV) and "abounding in the work of the Lord" (1 Corinthians 15:58). And what makes his life

---

[7] Richard Foster, "Heart to Heart: A Pastoral Letter from Richard J. Foster, November, 1996," *Renovaré*, p. 1 (newsletter mailed from 8 Inverness Dr. East, Suite 102, Englewood, Co 80112-5609).
[8] Ibid.

so powerful is that he pressed on in this passion under the immense struggles and hardships that he faced.

The Fruit of Brainerd's Affliction

We turn finally to the question, What was the fruit of Brainerd's affliction? First, I would mention the effect of Brainerd's life on Jonathan Edwards, the great pastor and theologian of Northampton, Massachusetts, in whose house Brainerd died at the age of twenty-nine. Edwards bears his own testimony:

> I would not conclude my observations on the merciful circumstances of Mr. Brainerd's death without acknowledging with thankfulness the gracious dispensation of Providence to me and my family in so ordering that he . . . should be cast hither to my house, in his last sickness, and should die here: So that we had opportunity for much acquaintance and conversation with him, and to show him kindness in such circumstances, and to see his dying behavior, to hear his dying speeches, to receive his dying counsel, and to have the benefit of his dying prayers. (p. 541)

Edwards said this even though he must have known it probably cost him the life of his eighteen-year-old daughter to have had Brainerd in his house with that terrible disease. Jerusha had tended Brainerd as a nurse for the last nineteen weeks of his life, and four months after he died she died of the same affliction on February 14, 1748. Edwards wrote,

> It has pleased a holy and sovereign God, to take away this my dear child by death, on the 14th of February . . .

after a short illness of five days, in the 18th year of her age. She was a person of much the same spirit with Brainerd. She had constantly taken care of and attended him in this sickness, for nineteen weeks before his death; devoting herself to it with great delight, because she looked on him as an eminent servant of Jesus Christ.[9]

So Edwards really meant what he said, that it was a "gracious dispensation of Providence" that Brainerd came to his house to die. He said it with full awareness of the cost.

A Pebble Dropped in the Sea of History

As a result of the immense impact of Brainerd's devotion on his life, Jonathan Edwards wrote, in the next two years, *The Life of David Brainerd*, which has been reprinted more often than any of his other books. And through this *Life* the impact of Brainerd on the church has been incalculable. Beyond all the famous missionaries who tell us that they have been sustained and inspired by Brainerd's *Life*,[10] how many countless other unknown faithful servants must there be who have found from Brainerd's testimony the encouragement and strength to press on!

It is an inspiring thought that one small pebble dropped in the sea of history can produce waves of grace that break on distant shores hundreds of years later and thousands of miles away. Robert Glover ponders this thought with wonder when he writes,

---

[9] Sereno Dwight, *Memoirs of Jonathan Edwards*, in *The Works of Jonathan Edwards*, vol. 1 (Edinburgh: The Banner of Truth Trust, 1974), p. xciv.

[10] For extended lists see Kilby, "David Brainerd: Knight of the Grail," pp. 197-203; John Thornbury, *David Brainerd: Pioneer Missionary to the American Indians* (Durham, England: Evangelical Press, 1996), pp. 298-300; Norman Pettit, "Editor's Introduction," in Jonathan Edwards, *The Life of David Brainerd*, pp. 3-4.

It was Brainerd's holy life that influenced Henry Martyn to become a missionary and was a prime factor in William Carey's inspiration. Carey in turn moved Adoniram Judson. And so we trace the spiritual lineage from step to step—Hus, Wycliffe, Francke, Zinzendorf, the Wesleys and Whitefield, Brainerd, Edwards, Carey, Judson, and ever onward in the true apostolic succession of spiritual grace and power and world-wide ministry.[11]

The Ironic Fruit of Failure

A lesser-known effect of Brainerd's life, and one that owes far more to the gracious providence of God than to any intention on Brainerd's part, was the founding of Princeton College and Dartmouth College. Jonathan Dickinson and Aaron Burr, who were Princeton's first leaders and among its founders, took direct interest in Brainerd's case at Yale and were extremely upset that the school would not readmit him. This event brought to a head the dissatisfaction that the New York and New Jersey Presbyterian Synods had with Yale and solidified the resolve to found their own school. The College of New Jersey (later Princeton) was chartered in October 1746. Dickinson was made the first president, and when the classes began in his house in May 1747 in Elizabethtown, Brainerd was there trying to recover his health in his last months. Thus he is considered to be the first student enrolled. David Field and Archibald Alexander and others testify

---

[11] Robert Glover, *The Progress of World-Wide Missions* (New York: Harper and Row, Publishers, 1952, orig. 1924), p. 56.

that in a real sense "Princeton college was founded because of Brainerd's expulsion from Yale" (p. 55).

Another surprising effect of Brainerd's life is the inspiration he provided for the founding of Dartmouth College by Eleazar Wheelock. Brainerd felt a failure among the Iroquois Indians on the Susquehanna. He labored among them for a year or so and then moved on. But his diary of the time kindled the commitment of Wheelock to go to the Iroquois of Connecticut. And inspired by Brainerd's example in teaching the Indians, he founded in 1748 a school for Indians and whites at Lebanon. Later it was moved to Hanover, New Hampshire, where Wheelock founded Dartmouth College (p. 62).

In 1740 Yale, Harvard, and William and Mary were the only Colonial colleges, and they were not sympathetic to the Evangelical piety of the Great Awakening. But the tide of Awakening brought in a zeal for education as well as piety, and the Presbyterians founded Princeton, the Baptists founded Brown, the Dutch Reformed founded Rutgers, and the Congregationalists founded Dartmouth. It is remarkable that David Brainerd must be reckoned as an essential motivational component in the founding of two of those schools. If he was a somewhat frustrated scholar, thinking and writing by candlelight in the wilderness,[12] his vision for evangelical higher education had a greater fulfillment probably than if he had given his life to that cause instead of to the missionary passion that he felt.

---

[12] Saturday, December 14. "Rose early and wrote by candlelight some considerable time" (p. 344).

Who Can Measure the Worth of a Worshiping Soul?

I close by stating that the most lasting and significant effect of Brainerd's ministry is the same as the most lasting and significant effect of every pastor's ministry. There are a few Indians—perhaps several hundred—who, now and for eternity, owe their everlasting life to the direct love and ministry of David Brainerd. Some of their stories would make another chapter—a very inspiring one. Who can describe the value of one soul transferred from the kingdom of darkness, and from the weeping and gnashing of teeth, to the kingdom of God's dear Son! If we live twenty-nine years or if we live ninety-nine years, would not any hardships be worth the saving of one person from the eternal torments of hell for the everlasting enjoyment of the glory of God?

My last word must be the same as Jonathan Edwards's. I thank God for the ministry of David Brainerd in my own life—the passion for prayer, the spiritual feast of fasting, the sweetness of the Word of God, the unremitting perseverance through hardship, the relentless focus on the glory of God, the utter dependence on grace, the final resting in the righteousness of Christ, the pursuit of perishing sinners, the holiness while suffering, the fixing of the mind on what is eternal, and finishing well without cursing the disease that cut him down at twenty-nine. With all his weaknesses and imbalances and sins, I love David Brainerd.

Perhaps his habit of writing is part of the reason I have continued to keep a journal over the last thirty-four years. From that journal—weak and worldly compared to Brainerd's—I recall that on June 28, 1986, my longtime associate and friend Tom Steller and his wife Julie and I visited Northampton, Massachusetts, in search of Brainerd's grave. I wrote:

This afternoon Tom and Julie and I drove to Northampton. We found the gravestone of David Brainerd, a dark stone slab the size of the grave top and a smaller white marble inset in the slab with these words:

> *Sacred to the memory of the*
> *Rev. David Brainerd. A faithful and*
> *laborious missionary to the*
> *Stockbridge, Delaware and Susquehanna*
> *TRIBES OF INDIANS WHO*
> *died in this town. October 10, 1747 AE 32*[13]

Tom and Julie (and their daughters Ruth and Hannah) and I took hands and stood around the grave and prayed to thank God for Brainerd and Jonathan Edwards and to dedicate ourselves to their work and their God. It was a memorable, and I hope, powerful and lasting moment.

Our prayer was then, and is now, that God would grant us a persevering grace to spread a passion for the supremacy of God in all things for the joy of all peoples. Life is too precious to squander on trivial things. Grant us, Lord, the unswerving resolve to pray and live with David Brainerd's urgency: "Oh, that I might never loiter on my heavenly journey!"

---

[13] Both these final facts are inaccurate: he died October 9 at the age of 29.

Jesus also suffered outside the gate

in order to sanctify the people through his own blood.

Therefore let us go forth to him outside the camp,

and bear the abuse he endured.

For here we have no lasting city,

but we seek the city which is to come.

HEBREWS 13:12-14, RSV

CONCLUSION

A Plea to Follow in the Fruitful Wake of the Suffering Swans

Ten thousand effects follow from every motion of your hand. The hidden mysteries of the chain of causation in the physical world is enough to hold us with amazement. How much more the ripple effect in the realm of persons and spirits! Clyde Kilby, who taught English literature at Wheaton College, pondered this in relation to David Brainerd and marveled:

> The pebble falling into the pond sends its waves onward until they are invisible, and yet in the mystery of the physical world, never end. If William Carey is stirred by David Brainerd, and if then John Newton, the great hymn writer, says that Carey is more to him than "bishop or archbishop: he is an apostle!" it is obvious that the waves are in motion. Or again if Adoniram Judson is inspired toward missionary labors in Burma through Carey, it is evident that the waves go onward.[1]

If William Cowper creates a cadence and a rhyme and a vision of reality on some dark day two hundred years ago, and then a brokenhearted church today sings "God Moves in a Mysterious Way" and hope awakens, the waves go on. If John Bunyan bends down and kisses his blind daughter, then walks back to his prison

---

[1] Clyde Kilby, "David Brainerd: Knight of the Grail," *Heroic Colonial Christians*, Russell T. Hitt, ed. (Philadelphia: J. B. Lippincott Company, 1966), pp. 201-202.

cell and writes a story that three centuries later, in Chinese, gives courage to an underground house-church pastor, the waves go on. How great are the wonders laid up for us in the God-wrought, sovereign sequences of history! "How unsearchable are his judgments and how inscrutable his ways!" (Romans 11:33, RSV).

The afflictions of John Bunyan and William Cowper and David Brainerd were not for naught. The pebbles did not drop in vain—neither in their own lifetimes, nor in the centuries to follow. God has breathed on the waters and made their ripples into waves. And now the parched places of our lives are watered with the memories of sustaining grace.

The Christian Life Is Hill Difficulty

Bunyan's life and labor call us to live like Pilgrim on the way to the Celestial City. His suffering and his story summon us, in the prosperous and pleasure-addicted West, to see the Christian life in a radically different way than we ordinarily do. There is a great gulf between the Christianity that wrestles with whether to worship at the cost of imprisonment and death, and the Christianity that wrestles with whether the kids should play soccer on Sunday morning. The full title of *The Pilgrim's Progress* shows the essence of the pilgrim path: "The Pilgrim's Progress from this World, to that Which is to Come: Delivered under the Similitude of a Dream wherein Is Discovered, the Manner of His Setting out, his Dangerous Journey, and Safe Arrival at the Desired Country." For Bunyan, in fact and fiction, the Christian life is a "Dangerous Journey."

The narrow way leads from the Wicket Gate to the Hill Difficulty.

The narrow way lay right up the hill, and the name of the going up the side of the hill is called *Difficulty*. Christian now went to the Spring, and drank thereof, to refresh himself (Isaiah 49:10), and then began to go up the Hill, saying,

> *The Hill, though high, I covet to ascend,*
> *The Difficulty will not me offend;*
> *For I perceive the Way to life lies here.*
> *Come, pluck up Heart, let's neither faint nor fear;*
> *Better, though difficult, the Right Way to go,*
> *Than wrong, though easy, where the End is Woe.*[2]

This is the Christian life for Bunyan—experienced in prison and explained in parables. But we modern, western Christians have come to see safety and ease as a right. We move away from bad neighborhoods. We leave hard relationships. We don't go to dangerous, unreached people groups.

Bunyan beckons us to listen to Jesus and his apostles again. Jesus never called us to a life of safety, nor even to a fair fight. "Lambs in the midst of wolves" is the way he describes our sending (Luke 10:3). "If they have called the head of the house Beelzebul, how much more will they malign the members of his household!" (Matthew 10:25). "He who loves his life loses it, and he who hates his life in this world will keep it to life eternal" (John 12:25). "Whoever of you does not renounce all that he has cannot be my disciple" (Luke 14:33, RSV).

The apostle Paul continues the same call: "Through many tribulations we must enter the kingdom of God" (Acts 14:22).

---

[2] John Bunyan, *The Pilgrim's Progress* (Uhrichsville, OH: Barbour and Company, Inc., 1990), p. 40.

We are "heirs of God and fellow heirs with Christ, if indeed we suffer with Him" (Romans 8:17). We should not be "moved by . . . afflictions . . . [since] this is to be our lot" (1 Thessalonians 3:3, RSV). Faith and suffering are two great gifts of God: "To you it has been granted for Christ's sake, not only to believe in Him, but also to suffer for His sake" (Philippians 1:29). The apostle Peter confirms the theme: "Do not be surprised at the fiery ordeal among you, which comes upon you for your testing, as though some strange thing were happening to you" (1 Peter 4:12). It isn't strange. It's normal. That is the message of *The Pilgrim's Progress*. The Hill Difficulty is the only path to heaven. There is no other. Suffering is as normal as a father disciplining a son. That is how the writer to the Hebrews describes the suffering of the saints: "God deals with you as with sons; for what son is there whom his father does not discipline? But if you are without discipline, of which all have become partakers, then you are illegitimate children and not sons" (Hebrews 12:7-8). The pattern is rooted in the Old Testament itself. So the psalmist says, "Many are the afflictions of the righteous" (Psalm 34:19; see Galatians 4:29).

Oh, how we need Bunyan! We are soft and thin-skinned. We are worldly; we fit far too well into our God-ignoring culture. We are fearful and anxious and easily discouraged. We have taken our eyes off the Celestial City and the deep pleasures of knowing God and denying ourselves the lesser things that titillate for a moment but then shrink our capacities for great joy. Bunyan's *Seasonable Counsel* for us is: Take up your cross daily and follow Jesus. "For whoever wishes to save his life will lose it; but whoever loses his life for My sake will find it" (Matthew 16:25).

Come, Wounded William Cowper, Teach Us How to Sing

The fruit of William Cowper's affliction is a call to free ourselves from trite and chipper worship. If the Christian life has become the path of ease and fun in the modern West, then corporate worship is the place of increasing entertainment. The problem is not a battle between contemporary worship music and hymns; the problem is that there aren't enough martyrs during the week. If no soldiers are perishing, what you want on Sunday is Bob Hope and some pretty girls, not the army chaplain and a surgeon.

Cowper was sick. But in his sickness he saw things that we so desperately need to see. He saw hell. And sometimes he saw heaven. He knew terror. And sometimes he knew ecstasy. When I stand to welcome the people to worship on Sunday morning, I know that there are William Cowpers in the congregation. There are spouses who can barely talk. There are sullen teenagers living double lives at home and school. There are widows who still feel the amputation of a fifty-year partner. There are single people who have not been hugged for twenty years. There are men in the prime of their lives with cancer. There are moms who have carried two tiny caskets. There are soldiers of the cross who have risked all for Jesus and bear the scars. There are tired and discouraged and lonely strugglers. Shall we come to them with a joke?

They can read the comics every day. What they need from me is not more bouncy, frisky smiles and stories. What they need is a kind of joyful earnestness that makes the broken heart feel hopeful and helps the ones who are drunk with trifles sober up for greater joys.

What William Cowper gives us from his suffering is a vision

that sustains the suffering church. Until we suffer we will not be interested. But that day is coming for all of us. And we do well not to wait until it comes before we learn the lessons of Cowper's great hymn "God Moves in a Mysterious Way":

> *Ye fearful saints, fresh courage take,*
> *The clouds ye so much dread*
> *Are big with mercy, and shall break*
> *In blessings on your head.*
>
> *Blind unbelief is sure to err,*
> *And scan his work in vain:*
> *God is his own interpreter,*
> *And He will make it plain.*

There is an entire theology of suffering in Cowper's hymns. It is sturdy and sound and redwood-like in the midst of our sapling sermonettes. Oh, how our people need to study and savor and sing the great God-centered truth of these verses! (For the entire hymn see Chapter Two.) How shall entertaining worship services— with the aim of feeling lighthearted and friendly—help a person prepare to suffer, let alone prepare to die? If we know how to suffer well, and if we feel that "to die is gain" because of Jesus, then we will know how to live well. We will know how to laugh— not mainly at jokes (which takes no more grace than a chair has) but at the future. "Strength and dignity are her clothing, and she laughs at the time to come" (Proverbs 31:25, RSV).

Worship is the display of the surpassing worth of God revealed in Jesus Christ. Suffering in the path of Christian obedience, with joy—because the steadfast love of the Lord is better than life (Psalm 63:3)—is the clearest display of the worth of God in our lives. Therefore, faith-filled suffering is essential in this world for the most intense, authentic worship. When we are most satisfied with God in suffering, he will be most glorified in us in worship. Our problem is not styles of music. Our problem is styles of life. When we embrace more affliction for the worth of Christ, there will be more fruit in the worship of Christ.

Oh, come, wounded William Cowper, and feed us on the fruit of your affliction. Teach us to study, savor, and sing your sacred songs of suffering joy.

One Passion: the Salvation of Sinners for the Glory of God

When we have learned from John Bunyan that the path to life leads up Hill Difficulty, and from William Cowper that earnest, joyful worship is the fruit of affliction, then let us learn from David Brainerd that a life devoted to the glory of Christ is a life devoted to the Great Commission. The fruit of Brainerd's affliction was the salvation of hundreds of Indians and the inspiration of thousands of missionaries. His suffering is the sound of a trumpet over all the unreached peoples of the world, pealing out the word of Christ: "All authority in heaven and on earth has been given to me. Go therefore and make disciples of all nations" (Matthew 28:18-19, RSV).

His suffering extends the shadow of the cross into our lives and bids us ask if we can say with Paul, "I am crucified with Christ" (Galatians 2:20, KJV). It echoes the single-minded passion of the apostle when he said, "I do not account my life of any value nor as precious to myself, if only I may accomplish my course and the ministry which I received from the Lord Jesus, to testify to the gospel of the grace of God" (Acts 20:24, RSV). It summons us from Calvary with the words of Hebrews 13:12-14, "Jesus also suffered outside the gate in order to sanctify the people through his own blood. Therefore let us go forth to him outside the camp, and bear the abuse he endured. For here we have no lasting city, but we seek the city which is to come" (RSV).

When you spend the last seven years of your life spitting up blood and die at age twenty-nine, you don't just say those words—"here we have no lasting city"—you feel them the way you feel the wind on a cliff's edge. Oh, how many feel the wind and run inland! The call of Christ and the call of Brainerd are exactly the opposite of such a retreat: Since we have no lasting city here, stop working so hard trying to make it lasting and luxurious, and "go forth to him outside the camp"—outside the safe place, outside the comfortable place. Yes, Golgotha is a bleak hill—a skull with a frown of affliction on its face. But remember: "Behind a frowning providence he hides a smiling face." Let go of what holds you back from full and radical service—be ready to suffer for finishing the Great Commission. Don't forget "that you have for yourselves a better possession and a lasting one" (Hebrews 10:34). You have God—and all that he is for you in Jesus.

"You will make known to me the path of life; in Your presence is fullness of joy; in Your right hand there are pleasures forever" (Psalm 16:11). The path to everlasting joy in God leads up Hill Difficulty, with deep and joyful worship, into an unreached world of perishing sinners, where the repentance of one soul sets the angels of God to singing. This is a fruit of affliction that will last forever and multiply all your joys in Christ.

A NOTE ON RESOURCES

DESIRING GOD MINISTRIES

If you would like to ponder further the vision of God and life presented in this book, we at Desiring God Ministries (DGM) would love to help you. DGM is a resource ministry of Bethlehem Baptist Church in Minneapolis, Minnesota. Our desire is to fan the flame of your passion for God and help you spread that passion to others. We have hundreds of resources available for this purpose. Most of our inventory consists of books and audiotapes by John Piper. We also maintain a large collection of free articles, sermon manuscripts, and audio messages at our web site. In addition, we produce God-centered children's curricula, host conferences, and coordinate John Piper's conference speaking schedule.

Since money is not our treasure we try to keep our prices as low as possible. And since we don't want money to be a hindrance to the Gospel, if our prices are more than you can pay at this time, our *whatever-you-can-afford* policy applies to almost all of our resources—even if you can't afford to pay anything! We also accept VISA, MasterCard, Discover, and American Express credit cards for convenience and speed, but we would rather give you resources than have you go into debt.

DGM exists to help you make God your treasure. Because God is most glorified in you when you are most satisfied in him.

For more information, call to request a free resource catalog or browse our online store at *www.desiringGOD.org*.

DESIRING GOD MINISTRIES
720 Thirteenth Avenue South
Minneapolis, Minnesota 55415-1793

Toll free in the USA: 1-888-346-4700
International calls: (612) 373-0651
Bethlehem Baptist Church: (612) 338-7653
Fax: (612) 338-4372
mail@desiring GOD.org
www.desiringGOD.org

DESIRING GOD MINISTRIES
UNITED KINGDOM
23 Ashburn Avenue
Waterside, Londonderry
Northern Ireland BT46 5QE

Tel/fax: (02871) 342 907
desiringGOD@UK-Europe.freeserve.co.uk

INDEX OF SCRIPTURES

INDEX OF PERSONS

INDEX OF SUBJECTS